Mangal Pandey

A Real Hero

Mangal Pandey

A Real Hero

Dr. Rakesh Kumar Pandey
Associate Professor & Head
Department of English,
National P.G. College,
Barahalganj, Gorakhpur (U.P)

Raj Publications
New Delhi-110002

Mangal Pandey: *A Real Hero*

First Published in 2018

₹ 795

ISBN 978-93-82281-92-4

Published by : **Raj Publications**
108, 4855/24, Ansari Road,
Daryaganj, New Delhi - 110002
Tel. : 011-23250939, 9811010939
E-Mail: rajpublications@yahoo.co.in

Laser Typesetting : Aarati Computers, Delhi-110 009

Printed at : Balaji Offset, Delhi

Contents

Preface

Mangal Pandey was born on 19 July 1827 in Nagwa, Ballia, Uttar Pradesh into a high-caste Bhumihar Brahmin family. His father Divakar Pandey was a peasant. Mangal Pandey had a sister who died during the famine of 1830. Pandey grew up to be an ambitious young man.

At Barrackpore on the afternoon of 29 March 1857, Lieutenant Baugh, Adjutant of the 34th Bengal Native Infantry (BNI), was informed that several men of his regiment were in an excited state. Further, it was reported to him that one of them, Mangal Pandey, was pacing in front of the regiment's guard room by the parade ground, armed with a loaded musket, calling upon the men to rebel and threatening to shoot the first European that he set eyes on. Baugh immediately buckled on his sword, placed loaded pistols in his holsters, mounted his horse, and galloped to the lines.

Pandey took position behind the station gun, which was in front of the quarter-guard of the 34th, took aim at Baugh and fired. He missed Baugh, but the bullet struck his horse in the flank, and horse and rider were brought down. Baugh quickly disentangled himself and, seizing one of his pistols, advanced towards Pandey and fired. He missed. Before Baugh could draw his sword, Pandey attacked him with a talwar (a heavy Indian sword) and closing with the adjutant, slashed Baugh on the shoulder and neck and brought him to the ground. It was then that another sepoy, Shaikh Paltu, intervened and tried to restrain Pandey even as he tried to reload his musket. All the matter is just compiled and edited in nature. Taken from the various sources which are in public domain.

Uncovering the hard facts behind the myths and conjectures of popular belief, nationalist rhetoric and cinematic imagination, this book provides, for the first time, a credible portrait of Mangal Pandey as he really was.

—Dr. Rakesh Kumar Pandey

1

Early Life

A sepoy working under the British East India Company, Mangal Pandey's name got etched into the pages of the Indian history after he attacked his senior British officers in an incident, which is today remembered as the Sepoy Mutiny of 1857 or the India's First War of Independence. The reason behind this was the rumor that the cartridges used by Indian sepoys were greased with the fat of cow and pig.

Mangal Pandey, whose name is often preceded by Shaheed meaning a martyr in Hindi, was an Indian soldier during the pre-independence era. A member of the 34th Regiment of the Bengal native infantry of the East India Company, Mangal Pandey is counted among the most popular figures associated with India's freedom struggle in present times. He was born on 19 July 1827 in the Nagwa village in the Ballia district of the Uttar Pradesh state. There still exist families in this village who claim to the descendents of Mangal Pandey.

However, some disputes exist over the exact place where Mangal Pandey was born. So read on to know more about the biography of Mangal Pandey, who joined the sepoy force of the British East India Company in the year 1849 at the age of 22. His name got etched into the pages of the Indian history after he attacked his senior British officers in an incident, which is today called the Sepoy Mutiny of 1857 or the India's First War of Independence. Due to this, he was later captured and hung till death on 8 April in 1857.

Here's more about the life history of Mangal Pandey, who was a devout Hindu and practiced his religion strictly. It was rumored that the cartridge used in the Enfield P-53 rifle which was being used by the Indian sepoys was greased with the fat of pig and cow fat. These cartridges had to be bitten off in order to remove the cover prior use and this went against the religious beliefs of the Muslims and Hindus. The general opinion was that the Britishers had deliberately done this to hurt the sentiments of Indians. And this was the main reason behind the outburst of Pandey's anger.

Mangal Pandey was an Indian soldier who played a major role in inciting the Indian rebellion of 1857. A sepoy serving with the British East India Company, he protested against the issue of greased cartridge to the soldiers; the cartridges were rumored to have been greased with either cow or pig lard. A staunch Hindu Brahmin, it was against his religious beliefs to bite off the ends of greased cartridges if they had indeed been lubricated with animal fat. Soon the belief rose among the soldiers that the British had deliberately used pig or cow fat, and Mangal Pandey incited the other soldiers to join him in a protest against the British. On 29 March 1857, he paced in front of the regiment's guard room by the parade ground, calling his fellow Indian soldiers to rebel. Armed with a musket, he attacked two Europeans, injuring them badly. Some of his fellow soldiers joined him in the rebellion though another sepoy, Shaikh Paltu, restrained Pandey in order to prove his loyalty to the British. In order to escape arrest Pandey tried to kill himself but failed. He was arrested and executed soon after. His death triggered off a series of mutinies by Indian soldiers in various parts of the country leading to what became known as the Indian rebellion of 1857.

Childhood

Mangal Pandey was born on 19 July 1827 in Nagwa, Balia, Uttar Pradesh into a high-caste Bhumihar Brahmin family. His father Divakar Pandey was a peasant. Mangal Pandey had a sister who died during the famine of 1830. Pandey grew up to be an ambitious young man.

Later Years

Mangal Pandey joined the army of the British East India Company in 1849 as a young man of 22 years. Some accounts suggest that his recruitment was a random event—he was recruited by a brigade that was marching past him while he was on a visit to Akbarpur.

He was made a soldier (sepoy) in the 6th Company of the 34th Bengal Native Infantry. Initially he was very excited about his military career which he considered to be a stepping stone for further professional success in future. There were also several other Brahmin young men in his regiment.

He, however, began to grow disenchanted with military life as the years passed. An incident that happened when he was posted at the garrison in Barrackpore in the mid-1850s would change the course of his life and significantly impact the Indian independence movement.

A new Enfield rifle was introduced into India and the cartridge was rumored to be greased with animal fat, primarily from pigs and cows. To use the rifle, the soldiers would have to bite off the ends of greased cartridges in order to load the weapon.

Since the cow is a holy animal to the Hindus, and the pig is abhorrent to Muslims, the use of fats from these animals was considered controversial by the Indian soldiers. The Indian troops thought that it was a deliberate act of the British in an attempt to defile their religions.

Mangal Pandey, a staunch Hindu Brahmin, was enraged by the alleged use of lard in the cartridges. He decided to take violent action against the British to show them his disapproval.

On 29 March 1857, Mangal Pandey, armed with a loaded musket, paced in front of the regiment's guard room by the parade ground, inciting the other Indian soldiers to revolt against the British. Several other men were with him. The Indian soldier planned to kill the first European he set his eyes on.

Lieutenant Baugh, Adjutant of the 34th Bengal Native Infantry (BNI), learned of the revolt and galloped on his horse to disperse the rebellious men. On seeing him approach, Pandey took position, aimed at Baugh and fired. The bullet missed the British officer but hit his horse, bringing them down.

Acting quickly Baugh sized a pistol and fired at Pandey. He missed. Pandey then attacked him with a talwar—a heavy Indian sword—and injured the European officer badly and brought him to the ground. At this crucial juncture, another Indian sepoy, Shaikh Paltu, intervened and tried to restrain Pandey.

By this time word reached the other British officers and Sergeant-Major Hewson arrived at the ground. He ordered Jemadar Ishwari Prasad, the Indian officer in command of the quarter-guard, to arrest Mangal Pandey, but Prasad refused to oblige.

Hewson then went to Baugh's aid, and was knocked to the ground from behind by a blow from Pandey's musket. Meanwhile Shaikh Paltu also tried to defend the two Englishmen. Many other sepoys stood watching the fight as mute spectators while a few advanced and hit the English officers.

More English officers arrived on the scene. Sensing that his arrest was inevitable, Mangal Pandey tried to kill himself. He shot himself in the chest and collapsed bleeding but was not fatally wounded. He was arrested and brought to trial.

Major Works

Mangal Pandey is best remembered for his revolt against the British officers on 29 March 1857 when he incited his fellow soldiers to join him in a rebellion against the Europeans. He managed to badly injure two English officers before he was arrested and sentenced to death. This incident is believed to have provoked Indian soldiers across the nation which led to a series of revolts all over the country in the ensuing weeks.

Persona Life & Legacy

After being arrested he was tried and sentenced to death. Some reports suggest that Mangal Pandey was under the influence of drugs—possibly cannabis or opium—at the time of the revolt and was not fully conscious of his actions.

His execution was set for 18 April 1857. The British authorities, however, feared the outbreak of a bigger revolt if they waited this long and executed him by hanging on 8 April 1857. Mangal Pandey's actions against the British triggered off a series of revolts all over India which ultimately culminated in the outbreak of the Indian rebellion of 1857.

He is considered to be a freedom fighter in India and the Indian government issued a postage stamp to commemorate him in 1984. Several movies and stage plays have been based on his life, including the Hindi film 'Mangal Pandey: The Rising' and the stage play titled 'The Roti Rebellion' in 2005.

The 1857 Incident

At Barrackpore on the afternoon of 29 March 1857, Lieutenant Baugh, Adjutant of the 34th Bengal Native Infantry (BNI), was informed that several men of his regiment were in an excited state. Further, it was reported to him that one of them, Mangal Pandey, was pacing in front of the regiment's guard room by the parade ground, armed with a loaded musket, calling upon the men to rebel and threatening to shoot the first European that he set eyes on. Baugh immediately buckled on his sword, placed loaded pistols in his holsters, mounted his horse, and galloped to the lines.

Pandey took position behind the station gun, which was in front of the quarter-guard of the 34th, took aim at Baugh and fired. He missed Baugh, but the bullet struck his horse in the flank, and horse and rider were brought down. Baugh quickly disentangled himself and, seizing one of his pistols, advanced towards Pandey and fired. He missed. Before Baugh could draw his sword, Pandey attacked him with a *talwar* (a heavy Indian sword) and closing with the adjutant, slashed Baugh on the shoulder and neck and brought him to the ground. It was then that another sepoy, Shaikh Paltu, intervened and tried to restrain Pandey even as he tried to reload his musket.

English Sergeant-Major Hewson, had arrived on the parade ground, summoned by a native officer, before Baugh. He had ordered Jemadar Ishwari Prasad, the Indian officer in command of the quarter-guard, to arrest Pandey. To this, the *jemadar* stated that his NCOs had gone for help and that he could not take Pandey by himself. In response Hewson ordered Ishwari Prasad to fall in the guard with loaded weapons. In the meantime, Baugh had arrived on the field shouting 'Where is he? Where is he?' Hewson in reply called out to Baugh, 'Ride to the right, sir, for your life. The sepoy will fire at you!' At that point Pandey fired.

Hewson had charged towards Pandey as he was fighting with Lieutenant Baugh. While confronting Pandey, Hewson was knocked to the ground from behind by a blow from Pandey's musket. The sound of the firing had brought other sepoys from the barracks; they remained mute spectators. At this juncture, Shaikh Paltu, while trying to defend the two Englishmen called upon the other sepoys to assist him. Assailed by other sepoys, who threw stones and shoes at his back, he called on the guard to help him hold Pandey, but they threatened to shoot him if he did not let go of the mutineer. Some of the sepoys of the quarter-guard then advanced and struck at the two prostrate officers. They then threatened Shaikh Paltu and ordered him to release Pandey, whom he had been vainly trying to hold back. However, Paltu continued to hold Pandey until Baugh and the sergeant-major were able to get up. Himself wounded by now, Paltu was obliged to loosen his grip. He backed away in one direction and Baugh and Hewson in another, while being struck with the butt ends of the guards' muskets.

In the meantime, a report of the incident had been carried to the commanding officer General Hearsey, who then galloped to the ground with his two officer sons. Taking in the scene, he rode up to the guard, drew his pistol and ordered them to do their duty by seizing Mangal Pandey. The General threatened to shoot the first man who disobeyed. The men of the quarter-guard fell in and followed Hearsey towards Pandey. Pandey then put the muzzle of the musket to his chest and discharged it by pressing the trigger with his foot. He collapsed bleeding, with his regimental jacket on fire, but not mortally wounded.

Pandey recovered and was brought to trial less than a week later. When asked whether he had been under the influence of any substances, he stated steadfastly that he had mutinied on his own accord and that no other person had played any part in encouraging him. He was sentenced to death by hanging, along with Jemadar Ishwari Prasad, after three Sikh members of the quarter-guard testified that the latter had ordered them not to arrest Pandey.

Mangal Pandey's execution was scheduled for 18 April, but was carried out ten days before that date. Jemadar Ishwari

Prasad was executed by hanging on 21 April.

Aftermath

The 34th B.N.I. Regiment was disbanded "with disgrace" on 6 May as a collective punishment, after an investigation by the government, for failing to perform their duty in restraining a mutinous soldier and their officer. This came after a period of six weeks while petitions for leniency were examined in Calcutta.

The Indian historian Surendra Nath Sen notes that the 34th B.N.I. had a good recent record and that the Court of Enquiry had not found any evidence of a connection with unrest at Berhampur involving the 19th B.N.I. four weeks before. However, Mangal Pandey's actions and the failure of the armed and on-duty sepoys of the quarter-guard to take action convinced the British military authorities that the whole regiment was unreliable. It appeared that Pandey had acted without first taking other sepoys into his confidence but that antipathy towards their British officers within the regiment had led most of those present to act as spectators rather than obey orders.

Motivation

The personal motivation behind Pandey's behaviour remains confused. During the incident itself he shouted to other sepoys: "come out - the Europeans are here"; "from biting these cartridges we shall become infidels" and "you sent me out here, why don't you follow me". At his court-martial he stated that he had been taking bhang and opium, and was not conscious of his actions on 29 March.

There were a wide range of factors causing apprehension and mistrust in the Bengal Army immediately prior to the Barrackpore event. Pandey's reference to cartridges is usually attributed to a new type of bullet cartridge used in the Enfield P-53 rifle which was to be introduced in the Bengal Army that year. The cartridge was thought to be greased with animal fat, primarily from cows and pigs, which could not be consumed by Hindus and Muslims respectively (the former a holy animal of the Hindus and the latter being abhorrent to Muslims). The cartridges had to be bitten at one end before use. The Indian troops in some regiments were of the opinion that this was an intentional act of the British, with the aim of defiling their religions.

Commandant Wheeler of the 34th BNI was known as a zealous Christian preacher. The wife of Captain William Halliday of the 56th BNI had the Bible printed in Urdu and Devanagari and distributed among the sepoys, thus raising suspicions amongst them that the British were intent on converting them to Christianity.

The 19th and 34th Bengal Native Infantry were stationed at Lucknow during the time of annexation of Oudh in 1856 because of alleged misgovernment by the Nawab. The annexation had negative implications for sepoys in the Bengal Army (a significant portion of whom came from that princely state). Before the annexation, these sepoys had the right to petition the British Resident at Lucknow for justice — a significant privilege in the context of native courts. As a result of the East India Company's action they lost that special status, since Oudah no longer existed as a nominally independent political entity.

The 19th B.N.I. is important because it was the regiment charged with testing the new cartridges on 26 February 1857. However, right up to the mutiny the new rifles had not been issued to them, and the cartridges in the magazine of the regiment were as free of grease as they had been through the preceding half century. The paper used in wrapping the cartridges was of a different colour, arousing suspicions. The non-commissioned officers of the regiment refused to accept the cartridges on 26 February. This information was conveyed to the commanding officer, Colonel Mitchell; he took it upon himself to try to convince the sepoys that the cartridges were no different from those they had been accustomed to and that they need not bite it. He concluded his exhortation with an appeal to the native officers to uphold the honour of the regiment and a threat to court-martial such sepoys as refused to accept the cartridge. However, the next morning the sepoys of the regiment seized their bell of arms (weapons store). The subsequent conciliatory behaviour of Mitchell convinced the sepoys to return to their barracks. A Court of Enquiry was ordered which, after an investigation lasting nearly a month, recommended the disbanding of the regiment. The same was carried out on 31 March. The 19th BNI were allowed to retain their uniforms and were provided by the Government with allowances to return to their homes.

Consequences

The attack by and punishment of Pandey is widely seen as the opening scene of what came to be known as the Indian Rebellion of 1857. Knowledge of his action was widespread amongst his fellow sepoys and is assumed to have been one of the factors leading to the general series of mutinies that broke out during the following months.

Film, Stage and Literature

A film based on the sequence of events that led up to the mutiny entitled *Mangal Pandey: The Rising* starring Indian actor, Aamir Khan along with Rani Mukerji, Toby Stephens and Amisha Patel, directed by Ketan Mehta was released on 12 August 2005.

The life of Pandey was the subject of a stage play titled *The Roti Rebellion*, which was written and directed by Supriya Karunakaran. The play was organized by Sparsh, a theatre group, and presented in June 2005 at The Moving Theatre at Andhra Saraswat Parishad, Hyderabad, Andhra Pradesh.

Samad Iqbal, a fictional descendant of Mangal Pandey, is

a central character in Zadie Smith's debut novel *White Teeth*. Pandey is an important influence on Samad's life and is repeatedly referenced and investigated by the novel's characters.

English Language

In the English language, Pandey is best remembered for the word his surname and his actions helped coin: *Pandy* — a traitor, particularly a rebellious sepoy of the Mutiny of 1857. Once a colloquial term widely used by English speakers in India, the word is now obsolete.

Commemoration

The Government of India commemorated Pandey by issuing a postage stamp bearing his image on 5 October 1984. The stamp and the accompanying first-day cover were designed by Delhi-based artist C. R. Pakrashi.

A park is named Shaheed Mangal Pandey Maha Udyan to commemorate the place where Pandey attacked British officers and was hanged, at Barrackpore road in Barrackpore sub-divisional town in North 24 Parganas district.

2

Barrackpore Mutiny of 1824

The Barrackpore mutiny was a rising of native Indian sepoys against their British officers in Barrackpore in November 1824. The incident occurred when the British East India Company was fighting the First Anglo-Burmese War (1824–26) under the leadership of the governor-general of India William Amherst, 1st Earl Amherst.

The mutiny had its roots in British insensitivity towards Indian cultural sentiments, combined with negligence and poor supply arrangements, which caused growing resentment amongst the sepoys of several regiments of the Bengal Native Infantry after a long march from Mathura to Barrackpore. The lack of transport for personal effects and cultural concerns about being transported by sea caused apprehension and when troops from the 47th Native Infantry appeared on parade, the troops refused to march towards Chittagong, unless their grievances were remedied. Attempts to resolve the dispute failed and dissent spread to elements of the 26th and 62nd Regiments. The Commander-in-Chief, India, General Sir Edward Paget, ordered the troops to lay down their arms before considering their requests for redress. When the sepoys refused, their camp was surrounded by loyal soldiers from the 26th and 62nd Regiments and two British regiments. After a final ultimatum, the camp was attacked with artillery and infantry and around 180 sepoys were killed, as were a number of civilian bystanders.

In the aftermath, a number of mutineers were hanged and others sentenced to long periods of penal servitude. The 47th Regiment was disbanded and its Indian officers dismissed, while its European officers were transferred to other regiments. The incident was largely suppressed in the media, with only limited information being released to the public but public outrage over the incident resulted in widespread condemnation of the British colonial government. Ordinary British people were especially furious with the government for its heavy-handedness in dealing with the sepoys' grievances.

Background

Prelude

During the First Anglo-Burmese War, in October 1824, the 26th, 47th and 62nd Regiments of the Bengal Native Infantry were ordered to march 500 mi (800 km) from Barrackpore, a military cantonment in Bengal near Calcutta, to Chittagong in preparation for entering Burmese territory. The regiments had just marched almost 1,000 mi (1,600 km) from Mathura to Barrackpore and were reluctant to undertake another long march, this time against the Burmese, an unknown enemy. Rumours of magical Burmese prowess spread amongst the Indian sepoys, affecting their morale. Moreover, these three regiments consisted mostly of high caste Hindus, who had reservations about crossing the sea due to the kala pani taboo.

Immediate Causes

Apart from fear and fatigue, what disheartened the sepoys the most was the absence of carriage cattle. Each high caste soldier used his own brass cooking utensils, wrapped in a bundle that also included his bedding. Because of their weight, the bundles could not be carried by the soldiers in addition to their knapsacks, muskets and ammunition. At the time, bullocks were generally used to pull the carts carrying the bundles. For the march to Chittagong, no bullocks could be found, since almost all the available animals had already been purchased for the sea-borne expedition to Rangoon. The few bullocks that were available were of inferior quality and cost exorbitant rates beyond the means of the sepoys, who requested that the government should provide the bullocks or pay them double batta (the allowance paid when in hostile territory) to cover the cost of purchasing them. These requests were disregarded and the sepoys were instead advised to carry whatever they could in their knapsacks and to leave the rest behind. To resolve the situation, commanding officers offered a 4,000 rupee advance to each regiment. The sepoys turned down this offer as it still meant paying baggage charges out of their own pocket. The situation was escalated by threats from a Muslim Indian Subedar Major, that if they did not stop complaining about the bullocks, they would be sent by sea.

Events of the Rebellion

The 26th Regiment was ordered to march first, followed by the 47th and then the 62nd Regiment. In a last moment change of orders, the 47th Regiment was asked to commence the march on November 1 1824, followed by the other two regiments who were ordered to start within a week of the 47th Regiment's departure. A parade was held on November 1, during which the soldiers of the 47th Native Infantry appeared without their knapsacks and refused to bring them even when ordered to do so. They again demanded their carriage bullocks or payment of double batta and refused to march without a redress of grievances. The commanding officer, General Dalzell, was unable to subdue the discontent and proceeded to Calcutta to consult the Commander-in-Chief, India, General Sir Edward Paget. The other two regiments were also affected and twenty Indian sepoys from the 26th BNI and 160 from the 62nd BNI defected to the refractory sepoys of the 47th Regiment.

Under the leadership of Bindee Tiwari, the sepoys maintained order during the day and stayed on the parade ground all night, while a petition was sent to Paget, who arrived from Calcutta on hearing of the escalation. Sepoys presented their demands to Paget via an emissary and explained that their act was due to religious scruples and requested to be dismissed from service, if the demands were not met. Paget replied that legitimate demands would only be addressed after the sepoys laid down their arms. This promise of reconsideration was not enough for the sepoys to give up their position. Paget, an old school martinet of Royal Service, considered this refusal an act of armed mutiny. He summoned two regiments of European troops, the 47th (Lancashire) Regiment of Foot and the 1st (Royal) Regiment, as well as troops of the Governor General's bodyguard from Calcutta. He also brought horse artillery from nearby Dum Dum. On the morning of November 2, the reinforcements and the loyal members of the 26th and 62nd Regiments moved into position. They secretly surrounded the sepoy camp ground and a final message was sent to the mutineers, demanding that they lay down arms before any discussion on grievances but it is said that only ten minutes were offered to make up their minds. The sepoys either hesitated or rejected the ultimatum and Paget ordered two cannons to fire on the rebels, followed by an attack from the rear by the secretly placed horse artillery. Surprised by this sudden assault, the sepoys tried to flee but the rest of the British regiments attacked from all directions.

Some of the sepoys jumped into the Hooghly River to escape and drowned, others entered local households for shelter but the loyalists chased them in and killed them with bayonets. Many bystanders, including women and children who happened to be in the neighbourhood, were killed during the operation. Afterwards, it was found that the muskets of the Indian sepoys were not loaded. Stevenson concludes that this implies no violence was intended by the rebels.

Casualties

Of about 1,400 mutineers, 180 were killed during the attack, although the death toll is disputed. Bengal Hurkaru, a local semi-official newspaper, published a report in November 1824, stating that the number of deceased was 100, per a "perfect guess". In 1827, Joseph Hume, an opposition MP, reported on the floor of the British Parliament that the number was from 400–600 per the "facts that had reached him from India". In response Charles Williams-Wynn, a Tory MP, claimed on behalf of the government, that the number was no more than 180.

Aftermath—Punishment of the Mutineers

Most of the remaining mutineers were captured and on November 2, eleven sepoys were identified as the ring leaders and received a swift trial, where they were sentenced to death by hanging. Six of these were from 47th BNI, four were from 62nd BNI and one was from 26th BNI, who were killed the same day in the parade ground. Around 52 sepoys were sentenced to fourteen years' hard labour, in chains, on roads; numerous others were sentenced with lesser terms. On November 4, by a general order issued from Fort William, the 47th Regiment was disbanded and its Indian officers disgraced, discharged and declared unworthy of the confidence of the government, as it was thought mutiny could not have occurred without their knowledge. All the British officers were transferred to a new 69th Regiment. On November 9, Bindee was arrested nearby, and suffered the especially harsh punishment of being hung in chains on the next day. His body was left to rot for months in open public display.

Press Censorship

The news of the unrest in Barrackpore, especially

concerning the use of violence to subdue a peaceful protest, was suppressed in public media in Calcutta, London and elsewhere. The colonial government maintained its silence except for a short official paragraph published in the *Calcutta Gazette* on November 4, where the incident was largely trivialised, with no mention of casualties. *Bengal Hurkaru,* a local semi-official newspaper under the editorship of a British Deputy Judge-Advocate, also published a short report in November 1824. The report played down the incident and lacked basic details including the cause of the mutiny, stating that they were not allowed to publish such details. Apart from these two reports, common Indians and Britons were largely kept uninformed about the incident, although rumours circulated.

Later Criticism in Press

The *Oriental Herald* in London first published a story on the subject almost six months after the incident, calling it the "Barrackpore Massacre", based on a report by a British correspondent in Calcutta. The *Oriental Herald* severely criticised British officers for the indiscriminate slaughter, Paget in particular for resorting to violence to suppress a peaceful protest, and demanded increased pay for the sepoys as well the provision of transport for luggage. It also sought a consistent and truthful account of the incident from the government. The report was particularly harsh in its criticism of Amherst, whom it labelled an "evil genius", blaming him for the escalation.

If this example was necessary to preserve the obedience of the native troops, how miserably precarious is the tenure of our authority! If it was not necessary, may God forgive those who have brought this stain upon British name. — *Barrackpore Massacre – Burmese War – Present State of the Native Army in Bengal, The Oriental Herald, Volume 5, 1825.*

Consequences

After the massacre, many sepoys deserted British service.

A Court of Inquiry was set up to investigate the incident. All that is known about its report was that it agreed that the sepoys had justifiable grievances. Bengal units designated for 'General Service' were given all the concessions that the rebellious sepoys had originally demanded. The 1824 incident created an atmosphere of distrust across the native Indian regiments and irrevocably harmed relations between British officers and native Indian sepoys.

No disciplinary measures were taken against Paget or any other officer of the army, contrary to expectations. Amherst came close to being recalled for mishandling the situation but ultimately retained his position.

Debate in British Parliament

On 22 March 1827, a parliamentary debate in the House of Commons discussed the Barrackpore Mutiny. Hume, a Radical MP from the opposition, described the incident to his colleagues, criticising the conduct of the military, and appealed for a fresh investigation to identify those responsible; he perceived that Amherst was showing a lack of will in finding the real culprits. He also alleged that the report of the Court of Inquiry was being suppressed, demanded that the full report be produced in Parliament, and appealed for the House to hear both sides of the dispute and come to a just conclusion. Tory MPs from the government side, such as Wynn and Davies, objected to the proposal and supported Amherst and Paget. At the end of the debate, the motion for a fresh investigation and the presentation of the inquiry's report to the House was defeated, 44 votes for the motion and 176 against.

Historical Significance

The Barrackpore cantonment was the site of another mutinous incident thirty-three years later on March 29, 1857 involving sepoy Mangal Pandey. The 1824 and 1857 mutinies had similar causes, including insensitivity of the British officers towards Indian cultural sensibilities. Both culminated in heavy-handed British repression, creating mass dissent and resentment among the sepoys. Because of the similarities, some British sources (including Encyclopedia Britannica) regard the 1824 mutiny as a "dress rehearsal" of the Indian Mutiny of 1857. The 24th Chief of Army Staff of the Indian Army, Major General V.K. Singh (2010–2012), wrote extensively about the 1824 Barrackpore mutiny. He reflects:

What shocked everyone was not the mutiny itself but the brutal manner in which it was quelled. The bloodshed could have been avoided if the situation had been handled with tact and understanding by the officers, particularly General Paget. Though the mutiny was quickly suppressed – it lasted for less than a day – its long term effects were far reaching and had a bearing on the Great Indian Mutiny of 1857.— *Gen V.K. Singh, Barrackpore Mutiny, Contribution of the Armed Forces to the Freedom Movement in India.*

The events of 1824 continued to haunt Britons and Indians for many years and many felt that it provided Indian sepoys the rationale to kill British officers in 1857.

Memorial

Bindee became a martyr and a fabled hero among the Indian sepoys especially after his death. To commemorate the incident, six months after Bindee's death, Indian sepoys and locals erected a temple near the site of his execution. Binda Baba temple as it is now known, still stands.

3

The Great Mutiny: India's First War of Freedom

Mangal Pandey laid the foundation stone for the freedom of India by his feathers and bold action against British rule. The profound hypocrisy and inherent barbarism of bourgeois civilization lies unveiled before our eyes, turning from its home, where it assumes respectable forms, to the colonies, where it goes naked. Did they not, in India, to borrow an expression of that great robber, Lord Clive himself, resort to atrocious extortion, when simple corruption could not keep pace with their rapacity? While they prated in Europe about the inviolable sanctity of the national debt, did they not confiscate in India the dividends of the rajahs, who had invested their private savings in the Company's own funds? While they combated the French revolution under the pretext of defending "our holy religion," did they not forbid, at the same time, Christianity to be propagated in India, and did they not, in order to make money out of the pilgrims streaming to the temples of Orissa and Bengal, take up the trade in the murder and prostitution perpetrated in the temple of the Juggernaut? These are the men of "Property, Order, Family, and Religion."

The story of the Sepoy (sepahi) War of 1857, (an attempt at a compromise between two more controversial titles, 'the Sepoy Mutiny of 1857' and 'the Sepoy Rebellion of 1857,' though "insurgency" might also fit) began long before March of 1857. The history of the war delves deep into the colonization and conquest of India and the cultural and religious oppression imposed on Indians by British rule.

Furthermore, the telling of the history of the war is, to this day, an ongoing battle between two competing narratives, the history belonging to the British that won the war, and the history claimed by the Indians who were defeated. In a time when the history of India is being retold everyday, this web page is an attempt to present a history of the Sepoy War that is derived from various points of view, accounting for the context of the histories related, and the points of view of the historians relating them.

The East India Company was a massive export company that was the force behind much of the colonization of India. The power of the East India Company took nearly 150 years to build. As early as 1693, the annual expenditure in political "gifts" to men in power reached nearly 90,000 pounds (Marx 23). In bribing the Government, the East India Company was allowed to operate in overseas markets despite the fact that the cheap imports of South Asian silk, cotton, and other products hurt domestic business. By 1767, the Company was forced into an agreement that is should pay 400,000 pounds into the National Exchequer annually. By 1848, however, the East India Company's financial difficulties had reached a point where expanding revenue required expanding British territories in South Asia massively. The Government began to set aside adoption rights of native princes and began the process of annexation of more than a dozen independent Rajes between 1848 and 1854 (Marx 51; Kaye 30). In an article published in The New York Daily Tribune on July 28, 1857, Karl Marx notes that "... in 1854 the Raj of Berar, which comprise 80,000 square miles of land, a population from four to five million, and enormous treasures, was forcibly seized" (Marx 51).

In order to consolidate and control these new holdings, a well-established army of 200,000 South Asians officered by 40,000 British soldiers dominated India by 1857. The last vestiges of independent Indian states had disappeared and the East India Company exported tons of gold, silk, cotton, and a host of other precious materials back to England every year.

Religion

Historians like J.A.B. Palmer and John Kaye trace the origins of the soldiers' rebellion at Meerut, in which South Asian soldiers rose up against their colonial officers, to the Lee-Enfield Rifle. It was developed at the Enfield arsenal by James P. Lee and fired a. 303 caliber ammunition that had to manually loaded before firing. Loading involved biting the end of the cartridge, which was greased in pig fat and beef tallow. This presented a problem for native soldiers, as pig fat is a haraam, or forbidden, substance to Muslims, and beef fat is, likewise, deemed inauspicious for certain Hindus. Thus, the revolt occurred as a reaction to this particular intrusion into Hindu and Muslim culture, and then caught on as a national rebellion. Palmer dramatically relates this discovery, according to Captain Wright, commanding the Rifle Instruction Depot:

Somewhere about the end of the third week in January 1857, a khalasi, that is to say a labourer, accosted a high Brahmin sepoy and asked for a drink of water from his lotah (water-pot). The Brahmin refused on the score of caste. The khalasi then said, "You will soon lose your caste, as ere long you will have to bite catridges covered with the fat of pigs and cows," or, it is added, "words to that effect." Furthermore, historians taking similar positions argue that British legislation that interfered with traditional Hindu or Muslim religious practices were a source of antagonism. Palmer and Kaye also argue throughout their respective work that the prohibition practices such as saathi (often transliterated "sati"), or the ritual suicide of widows on their husbands' funeral pyres, became a source of outrage. In other words, the growing intrusion of western culture became the impetus for rebellious soldiers, fearful that their culture was being annihilated.

The long-belaboured significance of the Lee-Enfield cartridge is challenged by the work of historians like Marx, Collier, Majumdar, Chaudhuri, and Malleson. These historians argue that the actions of soldiers at Meerut was the "last straw" for South Asians who had been victims of British cultural and class based oppression and antagonism, and discard the notion that religion played an overwhelmingly vital role in fomenting revolt. For them, the root causes of the insurgency cannot be traced to a single, well-defined set of events and causes, but rather stemmed from an on-going set of conflicts.

Divide and Conquer

Col. G.B. Malleson argues that forcing Western ideas on an Eastern people fundamentally backfired, and the "divide and conquer" tactics employed by the British in India ultimately sowed the seeds of the rebellion. He notes, "action of a different character... so dear to the untravelled Englishman, or forcing the ideas in which he has been nurtured upon the foreign people with whom he has brought into contact, assisted... to loosen the bonds of discipline, which, up to that period, had bound the [Sepoy] to his officer" (Malleson 8). In other words, the Sepoy soldiers found themselves constantly pit against their countrymen in an army governed by what common soldiers came to feel were outside influences.

In a colonial setting, this is the prime breeding ground for a coup, (or in this case, a revolt) because any soldier's allegiance is governed by competition with other soldiers in currying favour and accumulating power, not by discipline or obedience to the orders of superior officers, and he begins to affiliate himself with his own people rather than the military ethics forced on him.

Expansionism

Greater still was the influence of British expansionism on the Sepoy Rebellion. Richard Collier explains how rapidly increasing territorial conquest also intesified Indian unrest:

> *... these annexations were a source of discontent and anxiety to many people besides the sepoys. In eight years, Canning's predecessor, the despotic Lord Dalhousie, at 35 the youngest Governor-General India had ever known, had annexed over 250,000 square miles— an area three times the size of England and Ireland. The Punjab, Sattara, Nagpur— Dalhousie's hands had stretched out to embrace them all. 'An Indian Governor General,' stormed The Hindu Patriot, 'is chartered to destroy dynasties with a scratch of his quill.' Indignities were heaped upon crowned heads: the jewels of the Royal Family of Nagpur were publicly auctioned in Calcutta.*

Partcipating in the military conquest of local authorities, then, and having first-hand knowledge of the effects of British expansionism would have fomented resistance in the Sepoys.

Torture and Oppression

On August 28, 1857, Marx published an article in The New York Daily Tribune in order to "show that the British rulers of India are by no means such mild and spotless benefactors of the Indian people as they would have the world believe". Marx cites the official Blue Books — entitled "East India (Torture) 1855-57"— that were laid before the House of Commons during the sessions of 1856 and 1857. The reports revealed that British officers were allowed an extended series of appeals if convicted or accused of brutality or crimes against Indians. Concerning matters of extortion in collecting public revenue, the report indicates that officers had free reign of any methods at their disposal.

Torture became a financial institution in colonial India, and was challenged by a petition from the Madras Native Association presented in January of 1856. The petition was dismissed on the basis of a lack of evidence, despite the fact that, according to the Marx, "there was scarcely any investigation at all, the Commission sitting only in the city of Madras, and for but three months, while it was impossible, except in very few cases, for the natives who had comnplaints to make to leave their homes" (Marx 74). Marx also refers to Lord Dalhousie's statements in the Blue Books that there was "irrefragable proof" that various officers had committed "gross injustice, to arbitrary imprisonment and cruel torture".

In addition to torture, the Company levied extremely large taxes on the Indian people. Collier describes taxes as "a cynical outrage. A man could not travel twenty miles without paying toll at a river ferry, farmed out by the Company to private speculators. Land Tax, often demanded before the crop was raised, was made in quarterly instalments... the annual rent for an acre of land was 3s[hillings]., yet the produce of that acre rarely averaged 8s[hillings]. in value."

Marx's position, as illustrated by the introductory quote to this page, is that the Indians were victims of both physical and economic forms of class oppression by the British. In Marx's analysis, the clash between the soldiers and their officers is the inevitable conflict that is the result of capitalism and imperialism.

The Rebellion

The military history of the rebellion is straightforward. Prior to the "mutiny" at Meerut on May 9th, 1857, fires broke out on January 22nd near Calcutta. An incident occurred on February 25th of that year when the 19th regiment mutinied at Berhampore, and the 34th Regiment rebelled at Barrackpore on the 31st of March. At Berhampore, the regiment allowed one of it's men to advance with a loaded musket upon the parade-ground in front of a line and open fire on his superior officer; a battle ensued. April saw fires at Allahabad, Agra, an Ambala, but the spark that lit the powder keg went off on May 9th in Meerut.

Members of the 3rd regiment of light cavalry were awaiting sentencing and imprisonment for refusal to obey orders and put the Lee-Enfield. caliber cartridge into their mouths. Once imprisoned, the 11th and 20th cavalry assembled and broke rank and turned on their commanding officers. After liberating the 3rd regiment, chaos ensued in Meerut, and the rebels engaged the remaining British Troops. Meerut was the single-most evenly balanced station in India in terms of the numbers of British and Indian soldiers. Troops and rebels were on near-even terms with 2,028 European Troops versus 2,357 sepoys, which certainly made the British side's capacity to defend its interest and defeat the Sepoys that much more likely. Furthermore, the British had 12 field guns and the sepoys had no artillery. Both Collier and Marx indicate that the rebellion would have ended there had Major-General William Hewitt cut off the rebel army at the bridge between Meerut and Delhi, some 40 miles away, with added weapons.

As the 38th, 54th, and 74th regiments of infantry and native artillery under Bakht Khan (c.1797- c.1859) joined the rebel army at Delhi in May. June 1857 marked the battle of Kanpur. The last Maratha prince, Baji Rao II, decreed his title and 80,000 pound annual pension to his son Nana Sahib (c.1820-c.1859) and was refused twice. Despite Sahib's attempts to push his claim, Lord Dalhousie refused the Hindu nobleman. Thus, in June 1857, Nana Sahib led the sepoy battalions at Crawnpore against the British. Nana Sahib sent word to Sir Hugh Wheeler, commander of the Britsh forces at Kanpur warning of the attack, guaranteeing him safe passage. On June 27, Nana Sahib broke the pact and trapped Wheeler in his palace. The events leading up to Wheeler's surrender and death have been recorded as the Kanpur Massacre.

The Kanpur Massacres

In the words of Sir Colin Campbell, leader of the British forces during the war: never was devised a blacker scheme than that which Nana Sahib had planned. Our miserable countrymen were conducted faithfully enough to the boats-officers, men, women, and children. The men and officers were allowed to take their arms and ammunition with them, and were escorted by nearly the whole of the rebel army. It was about eight o'clock a.m. when all reached the riverside-a distance of a mile and a half. Those who embarked first pushed off from the shore; but others found it difficult to get their boats off the banks, as the rebels had placed them as high as possible. At this moment the report of three guns was heard from the Nena's camp. The mutineers suddenly levelled their muskets, guns opened from the banks, and the massacre commenced. Some of the boats were set on fire, volley upon volley was fired upon the poor fugitives, numbers of whom were killed on the spot... A few boats crossed over to the opposite bank, but there a regiment of native infantry (the 17th), just arrived from Azimghur, was waiting for them; and in their eagerness to slay the "Kaffirs," rode their horses belly deep into the river to meet the boats, and hack our unhappy country men and women to pieces.

Andrew Ward's historical narrative, Our Bones Are Scattered, also relates an account of the terrible and bloody massacre that followed the rebellion at Kanpur, as well as Delhi and Meerut. By July, when Nana Sahib had captured Gwalior, he was reinstated as prince.

The Siege of Delhi

The siege of Lucknow lasted roughly from July 1st to August 31st. The commanding British officer, Sir Henry Lawrence, died early on during the siege. By July 25th two-thirds of the British forces had retreated across the river and Delhi had been taken by early September. Bahadur Shah, the last surviving Mogul ruler was installed as ruler and the devastating battle between rebel and British forces for control Delhi ensued. Soldiers faced down the horrific sight of the impregnable walls of Delhi and "more than fifty guns and mortars belching fire at Delhi's northern walls from the water bastion on the east to the Mori bastion on the west."

As the siege wore on the Punjabi forces fighting for the British began to weary and there was talk of a retreat. Under General John Nicholas, Delhi had toppled by September 20th, at the cost of 3,835 soldiers, British and Indian, and 378 horses (Collier 264). Rebel forces retreated to Lucknow where the siege was approaching three months in length. There the war lasted until late November, until the rebels were driven to defeat in the Ganges Valley in December and January by Hugh Rose and Colin Campbell. By July 8, 1858, a peace treaty was signed and the war ended. By 1859, Rebel leaders Bahkt Khan and Nana Sahib had been slain in battle.

Conclusion

Though the Sepoy War has been dismissed as a chaotic, disorganized peasant uprising, several facts go undisputed that offer a counter-argument. The "unorganized peasants" of India fought one of the most powerful empires in the world to near defeat with limited resources and even more limited training. Nevertheless, the lesson of the Sepoy War is not one of victory or justice, but failure.

Though the exact cause of the Sepoy War has yet to be agreed upon, and it is likely that there were many complex causes rather than one, it is clear that British interference governments and the oppression of the Indian people, religious and economic, created a bloody revolution. If there is a lesson to be learned from any of this, it is that a people, once pushed into a corner, will fight for nothing more than the freedom to fight, and live, if not for religion then for their basic right to live in freedom. Furthermore, in the desperate vengeance of a people reduced to pure indignity, lives a coldness that rivals that of their oppressors.

In the Footsteps of Mangal Pandey

It could have been any ordinary Sunday in the cantonment of Barrackpore. The month was March, and odd time in terms of the weather in Bengal. It was nearly the end of spring. It was hot but summer was still a few weeks away. In the early morning and after sunset a cool breeze came in from the river...

The sepoy lines in Barrackpore were quiet during the afternoon of 29 March in 1857. Most of the sepoys were lounging around, and the white officers were in their bungalows enjoying their siesta before preparing to go out with their families to attend evensong. Nobody anticipated that the serenity was about to be disrupted and history about to be made.

In the late afternoon, a sepoy of the 34th Native Infantry, wearing his regimental jacket but in a dhoti instead of the regulation trousers, appeared before the quarter-guard. It was obvious that he was greatly agitated. He had with him a loaded musket and his talwar. He belonged to the 5th Company and his name was Mangal Pandey. He strode around in the quarter-guard, shouting to his comrades. He asked the bugler to sound the assembly and yelled at his comrades to join him: "Come out, the Europeans are here! Why aren't you getting ready? It's for our religion! From biting these cartridges we shall become infidels. Get ready! Turn out, all of you! You have incited me to do this and now you ***, you will not follow me!" This kind of open insolence was not common among sepoys, and a naik quickly carried the report of Mangal Pandey's disorderly conduct to Sergeant-Major James Hewson. The naik, in his report to his white superior officer, added that Mangal Pandey was under the influence of bhang.

In a few minutes, Hewson was dressed and was at the parade ground. He summoned the jemadar of the company and demanded to know why the sepoy had not been arrested. The jemadar explained his helplessness, "What can I do?" he said. "The naik has gone to the adjutant. The havildar is gone to the field officer. Am I to take him myself?" Hewson ordered him to fall in his guard with loaded weapons. Hewson later recalled that some of the men grumbled and that the jemadar did not insist on the men falling in or loading. As the sergeant-major approached Mangal Pandey, the latter took aim and fired. The ball missed Hewson who took shelter behind the bell-of-arms (a bell-shaped building where weapons were stored). A couple of sepoys tried to persuade Mangal Pandey to surrender his weapons. By this time, the adjutant, Lieutenant Baugh, had arrived on horseback. The incident was now poised to take an even more dramatic turn.

Baugh galloped into the quarter-guard shouting, "Where is he? Where is he?" He was warned by Hewson, "To your left! Ride to the right, Sir, for your life. The sepoy will fire at you!" Mangal Pandey did exactly that and hit Baugh's horse, which collapsed. Baugh extricated himself, drew one of his pistols from the saddle holster and ran towards Mangal Pandey who was reloading his musket. Baugh fired from around 20 yards and missed. He then drew his sword and rushed towards the sepoy. According to Baugh's recollection, he had proceeded about halfway when Mangal Pandey drew his talwar. Baugh looked back to see where his horse was as he wanted to get his other pistol but the animal had wandered off. He decided to engage the sepoy and he was joined by Hewson, sword in hand...

Baugh, in his turn, had received a cut on his left hand, which disabled it. He had another deep cut on his neck and a gash on the back of his head from a musket butt. More serious harm to Baugh and Hewson was prevented by Sheikh Paltu, a Muslim sepoy, who held Mangal Pandey by his waist while the British officers escaped from what could have been their deaths. The saviour of Baugh and Hewson released

Mangal Pandey only when members of the quarter-guard threatened to shoot him if he did not let go of Mangal Pandey.

His actions created a name for the mutinous sepoys: British officers called them Pandies The commanding officer of the 34th Native Infantry, Steven Wheler, now appeared in the parade-ground. He ordered the jemadar to arrest the defiant sepoy. The jemadar replied, "The men won't go." Wheler repeated the order twice and the jemadar told his men to advance. They proceeded a few pace, stopped and refused to go any further. Wheler realised the futility of trying to enforce his order...

By now the news of the commotion in the parade ground had reached Major-General John Hearsey who commanded the Presidency Division. The General asked why the sepoy had not been arrested and he was told that the guard would not take orders... Hearsey then rode up to the quarter-guard. He pointed his pistol at the jemadar and said, "The first man who refuses to march when I give the word is a dead man. Quick march!" He then went towards Mangal Pandey; the guard followed while his sons covered the jemadar with their pistols. It was now Mangal Pandey's turn to act. This is what he did, in the words of Hearsey:

"It appeared the mutineer had suddenly altered his mind, I suppose seeing there was no chance of escape... He turned the musket muzzle towards his own breast hurriedly, touching the trigger with his toe. The muzzle must have swerved, for the bullet made a deep graze, ripping up the muscles of the chest, shoulder and neck, and he fell prostrate; we were on him at once. The guard calling out — 'He has shot himself.' A Sikh sepoy of the guard took his bloody tulwar from under him, for in falling he partly covered his sword with his body. His regimental jacket and clothes were on fire and smoking. I bid the jemadar and the sepoy to put the fire out, which they did... Dr Hutchinson being present, it was soon ascertained that the wound, though severe, was superficial, and the man was conveyed to the hospital."

One could say that as Mangal Pandey left the parade ground for the hospital, he moved away from history into myth. He did not die of his wounds. He was tried. the verdict was a foregone conclusion. He was hanged a few days later, on April 8. His actions created a name for the mutinous sepoys of 1857: the British officers called them Pandies.

One incident on a fateful Sunday in March. Was it linked to what was to happen in north India in the summer of the same year? Who was Mangal Pandey and why did he act the way he did? What were the cartridges that he had spoken about? Why did he say he was acting for 'our religion'?

Even one hundred and forty-eight years after the event and after a considerable amount of research on the subject, we have little or no precise knowledge about Mangal Pandey. There is a name and there is an action. There is no record about where he came from. Who were his parents? Was he married? When was he recruited and by whom? Answers to all these questions are unknown and speculative. Mangal Pandey has no curriculum vitae to put up to the

board of history. He could have preserved this anonymity, like innumerable other sepoys, had he not shot at his superior officers in Barrackpore. His was an unexpected intrusion into history.

4

First War of Indian Independence

The First war of Indian Independence was a period of rebellions in northern and central India against British power in 1857–1858. The British usually refer to the rebellion of 1857 as the Indian Mutiny or the Sepoy Mutiny. It is widely acknowledged to be the first-ever united rebellion against colonial rule in India.

Mangal Pandey, a Sepoy in the colonial British army, was the spearhead of this revolt, which started when Indian soldiers rebelled against their British officers over violation of their religious sensibilities. The uprising grew into a wider rebellion to which the Mughal Emperor, Bahadur Shah, the nominal ruler of India, lent his nominal support. Other main leaders were Rani Lakshmibai of Jhansi and Tantia Tope. The British cruelly put down the uprising, slaughtering civilians indiscriminately.

The result of the uprising was a feeling among the British that they had conquered India and were entitled to rule. The Mughal Emperor was banished and Queen Victoria of the United Kingdom was declared sovereign. The British East

India Company, which had represented the British Government in India and which acted as agent of the Mughals, was closed down and replaced by direct control from London through a Governor-General.

Prior to the revolt, some British officials in India saw Indians as equals and dreamed of a long-term partnership between Britain and India to the benefit of both. These officials had a sympathetic knowledge of Indian languages and culture. Afterwards, fewer officials saw value in anything Indian and many developed a sense of racial superiority, depicting India as a chaotic and dangerous place where the different communities, especially Muslim and Hindu, were only kept from butchering one another by Britain's exercise of power.

The rebellion was widely perceived to have been a mainly Muslim uprising, although prominent Hindus also participated. However, Muslims especially would find themselves less favored following this incident, with a few exceptions. India's eventual partition into India and Pakistan, based on the "two nation" theory that her Hindus and Muslims represented two distinct nations whose people could not live together in peace, may be seen as another long-term result of the uprising.

In British memory, novels and films romanticize the event extolling the bravery of their soldiers, while in Indian memory rebels such as Rani Lakshmi Bai and Nana Sahib enjoy the status of a Joan of Arc or of a William Wallace, fighting injustice.

Causes of the Revolt

Prior to the revolt, it is strictly speaking inaccurate to speak of British rule in India. The legal status of the East India Company was as agent of the Mughul Emperor with taxation powers and trading privileges. *De facto,* however, within the Province of Bengal, they operated as the Government and indeed the senior British official was entitled "Governor-General." Through a series of treaties with surrounding Indian princes and rulers, the Company extended its power throughout huge tracts of Indian territory. One cause of the revolt was the Company's policy of annexing Princely states with which they enjoyed a treaty relationship when they decided that the ruler was corrupt, or because they did not recognize the heir to the throne (such as an adopted son, who could succeed under Hindu law but not British law). There was also a rumor that Britain intended to flood India with Christian missionaries, and that pork and beef grease was being used to oil the new Enfield rifle that had been issued to the Indian troops. The latter appears to have been what motivated both Hindu and Muslim Sepoys (that is, Indian soldiers of the Company) to revolt.

In the year 1857, the British Army inducted a new type of rifle, the *Enfield,* whose cartridge was said to be greased in cow and pig fat. Hindus consider the cow a sacred animal and refrain from eating beef, while Muslims consider it an offense to consume pork. The entire Indian faction of the British Army rose in rebellion against the British. Soon, the flames spread and it turned into a full-fledged rebellion.

The "Doctrine of Lapse"

Under the "Doctrine of Lapse" policy of Lord Dalhousie (Governor-General 1846-1856) many kingdoms like Jhansi, Awadh or Oudh, Satara, Nagpur and Sambalpur were annexed turning the heirs of these kingdoms into 'pensioners' overnight. Nobility, feudal landholders, and royal armies found themselves unemployed and humiliated. These people were ready to avenge the injustice at the hands of the British. In addition the Bengal army of the East India Company drew many recruits from Awadh. They could not remain unaffected by the discontent back home. The jewels of the royal family of Nagpur were publicly auctioned in Calcutta, a move that was seen as a sign of abject disrespect by the remnants of the Indian aristocracy.

Indians were unhappy with the heavy-handed rule of the Company which had embarked on a project of rather rapid expansion and Westernization. This included the outlawing of many religious customs, both Muslim and Hindu, which were viewed as uncivilized by the British. This included a ban on sati (widow burning)—though it should be noted that the Sikhs had long ago abolished *sati* and the Bengali reformer Ram Mohan Roy was campaigning against it. These laws caused outrage in some quarters, particularly amongst the population of Bengal. The British abolished child marriage, and claimed to have ended female infanticide, but this claim is doubtful without accompanying demographic data. The suppression of *Thuggee* was a less controversial reform, although the true nature of Thuggee (whether it was truly a widespread religious cult, or simply dacoity) is still disputed.

The justice system was considered inherently unfair to the Indians. In 1853, the British Prime Minister Lord Aberdeen opened the Indian Civil Service to native Indians; however, this was viewed by some of educated India as an insufficient reform. The official Blue Books—entitled *"East India (Torture) 1855–1857"*—that were laid before the British House of Commons during the sessions of 1856 and 1857, revealed that Company officers were allowed an extended series of appeals if convicted or accused of brutality or crimes against Indians. The Company also practiced financial extortion through heavy taxation. Failure to pay these taxes almost invariably resulted in appropriation of property.

The British policy of expansionism (the Doctrine of Lapse) was also greatly resented by the rulers who were displaced, and outraged many if not most of their subjects, particularly in Oudh. In eight years Lord Dalhousie, the then Governor-General of India, had annexed a quarter of a million square miles (650,000 km^2) of land to the Company's territory.

Many of the Company's modernization efforts were viewed with automatic distrust; for example, it was feared that the railway, the first of which began running out of Bombay in the 1850s, was a demon.

However, some historians have suggested that the impact of these reforms has been greatly exaggerated, as the British did not have the resources to enforce them, meaning that away from Calcutta their effect was negligible. This was not the view taken by the British themselves after 1857: instead they scaled down their program of reform, increased the racial distance between Europeans and native Indians, and also sought to appease the gentry and princely families, especially Muslim, who had been major instigators of the 1857 revolt. After 1857, Zamindari (regional feudal officials) became more oppressive, the Caste System became more pronounced, and the communal divide between Hindus and Muslims became marked and visible, which some historians argue was due in great part to British efforts to keep Indian society divided. This tactic has become known as "divide and rule."

Start of the Revolt

Several months of increasing tension and inflammatory incidents preceded the actual rebellion. Fires, possibly the result of arson, broke out near Calcutta on January 24, 1857. On February 26, 1857, the 19th Bengal Native Infantry (BNI) regiment came to know about new cartridges and refused to use them. Their Colonel confronted them angrily with artillery and cavalry on the parade ground, but then accepted their demand to withdraw the artillery, and cancel the next morning's parade.

On March 29, 1857 at the Barrackpore (now *Barrackpur*) parade ground, near Calcutta, Mangal Pandey of the 34th BNI attacked and injured the adjutant Lt. Baugh with a sword after shooting at him, but instead hitting his horse. General John Hearsey came out to see him on the parade ground, and claimed later that Mangal Pandey was in some kind of "religious frenzy." He ordered a Jemadar Ishwari Prasad to arrest Mangal Pandey, but the jemadar refused. The whole regiment with the single exception of a soldier called Shaikh Paltu drew back from restraining or arresting Mangal Pandey.

Mangal Pandey, after failing to incite his comrades into an open and active rebellion, tried to take his own life by placing his musket to his chest, and pulling the trigger with his toe. He only managed to wound himself, and was court-martialed on April 6. He was hanged on April 8. The Jemadar Ishwari Prasad too was sentenced to death and hanged on April 22. The whole regiment was disbanded - stripped of their uniforms because it was felt that they harbored ill-feelings towards their superiors, particularly after this incident. Shaikh Paltu was, however, promoted to the rank of Jemadar in the Bengal Army. Sepoys in other regiments thought this a very harsh punishment. The show of disgrace while disbanding contributed to the extent of the rebellion in view of some historians, as disgruntled ex-sepoys returned home back to Awadh with a desire to inflict revenge, as and when the opportunity arose. April saw fires at Agra, Allahabad and Ambala.

3rd Light Cavalry at Meerut

On May 9, 85 troopers of the 3rd Light Cavalry at Meerut refused to use their cartridges. They were imprisoned, sentenced to ten years of hard labor, and stripped of their uniforms in public. It has been said that the town prostitutes made fun of the manhood of the sepoys during the night and this is what goaded them. This claim is however not substantiated by historical accounts. Malleson records that the troops were constantly berated by their imprisoned comrades while processing on a long and humiliating march to the jail. It was this insult by their own comrades which provoked the mutiny. The sepoys knew it was very likely that they would also be asked to use the new cartridges and they too would have to refuse in order to save their caste, religion and social status. Since their comrades had acted only in deference to their religious beliefs the punishment meted out by the British colonial rulers was perceived as unjust by many.

When the 11th and 20th native cavalry of the Bengal Army assembled in Meerut on May 10, they broke rank and turned on their commanding officers. They then liberated the 3rd Regiment and attacked the European cantonment where they are reported to have killed all the Europeans they could find, including women and children, and burned their houses. There are however some contemporary British accounts that suggest that some sepoys escorted their officers to safety and then rejoined their mutinous comrades. In Malleson's words: "It is due to some of them [sepoys] to state that they did not quit Meerut before they had seen to a place of safety those officers whom they most respected. This remark applies specially to the men of the 11th N.I., who had gone most reluctantly into the movement. Before they left, two sipáhís of that regiment had escorted two ladies with their children to the carabineer barracks. They had then rejoined their comrades". Some officers and their families escaped to Rampur, where they found refuge with the Nawab. Despite this, at the time wild rumours circulated about the complete massacre of all Europeans and native Christians at Meerut, the first of many such stories which would lead British forces to extremely violent reprisals against innocent civilians and mutinous sepoys alike during the later suppression of the revolt.

The rebellious forces were then engaged by the remaining British forces in Meerut. Meerut had the largest percentage of British troops of any station in India: 2,038 European troops with 12 field guns versus 2,357 sepoys lacking artillery. Some commentators believe that the British forces could have stopped the sepoys from marching on Delhi, but the British commanders of the Meerut garrison were extraordinarily slow in reacting to the crisis. They did not even send immediate word to other British cantonments that a rebellion was in process. It seems likely that they believed they would be able to contain the Indians by themselves. This misjudgment would cost them dearly.

Support and Opposition

The rebellion now spread beyond the armed forces, but

it did not result in a complete popular uprising as its leaders hoped. The Indian side was not completely unified. While Bahadur Shah Zafar was restored to the imperial throne there was a faction that wanted the Maratha rulers to be enthroned as well, and the Awadhis wanted to retain the powers that their Nawab used to have.

The war was mainly centered in northern and central areas of India. Delhi, Lucknow, Cawnpore, Jhansi, Bareilly, Arrah and Jagdishpur were the main centers of conflict. The Bhojpurias of Arrah and Jagdishpur supported the Marathas. The Marathas, Rohillas and the Awadhis supported Bahadur Shah Zafar and were against the British.

There were calls for jihad by some leaders including the millenarian Ahmedullah Shah, taken up by the Muslims, particularly Muslim artisans, which caused the British to think that the Muslims were the main force behind this event. In Awadh, Sunni Muslims did not want to see a return to Shiite rule, so they often refused to join what they perceived to be a Shia rebellion. Sir William Muir, the civil servant and scholar who later became Lt. Governor of the North West Provinces was head of intelligence during the rebellion, and recorded many details of the conflict in his Records of the NWP Intelligence Department (1902). From Agra, where he and his fellow British took refuge in the Red Fort, he wrote:

The Muslims defied our government in the most insolent manner. All the ancient feelings of warring for the faith reminding one of the first caliphs were resurrected. Few of the families who were otherwise strongly loyal to us could resist the temptation (46f).

In Thana Bhawan, the Sunnis declared Haji Imdadullah their Ameer. In May 1857 the famous Battle of Shamli took place between the forces of Haji Imdadullah and the British.

Many Indians supported the British, partly due to their dislike at the idea of return of Mughal rule and partly because of the lack of a notion of *Indianness.* The Sikhs and Pathans of the Punjab and North-West Frontier Province supported the British and helped in the capture of Delhi.

The Sikhs wanted to avenge the annexation of Punjab 8 years ago by the British with the help of Purbhais (Bengali's and Marathi's - Easterner) who helped the British. The Gurkhas of Nepal continued to support the British as well, although Nepal remained an independent country throughout the rebellion. Most of southern India remained passive with only sporadic and haphazard outbreaks of violence. Most of the states did not take part in the war as many parts of the region were ruled by the Nizams or the Mysore royalty and were thus not directly under British rule. The Westernized intellectuals felt that English rule would modernize and democratize the country and supported the foreigners.

Initial Stages

Bahadur Shah Zafar proclaimed himself the Emperor of the whole of India. Most contemporary and modern accounts however suggest that he was coerced by the sepoys and his courtiers - against his own will - to sign the proclamation. The civilians, nobility and other dignitaries took the oath of allegiance to the Emperor. The Emperor issued coins in his name, one of the oldest ways of asserting Imperial status, and his name was added to the Khutbah, the acceptance by Muslims that he is their King.

Initially, the Indian soldiers were able to significantly push back Company forces. The sepoys captured several important towns in Haryana, Bihar, Central Provinces and the United Provinces. The British forces at Meerut and Ambala held out resolutely and withstood the sepoy attacks for several months.

The British proved to be formidable foes, largely due to their superior weapons, training, and strategy. The sepoys who mutinied were especially handicapped by their lack of a centralized command and control system.

Rao Tularam of Haryana along with Pran Sukh Yadav fought with British Army at Nasibpur and then went to collect arms from Russia which had just been in a war with the British in the Crimea, but he died on the way. When a tribal leader from Peshawar sent a letter offering help, the king replied that he should not come to Delhi because the treasury was empty and the army had become uncontrollable.

Delhi

The British were slow to strike back at first but eventually two columns left Meerut and Simla. They proceeded slowly towards Delhi and fought, killed, and hanged numerous Indians along the way. At the same time, the British moved regiments from the Crimean War, and diverted European regiments headed for China to India.

After a march lasting two months, the British fought the main army of the rebels near Delhi in Badl-ke-Serai and drove them back to Delhi. The British established a base on the Delhi ridge to the north of the city and the siege began. The siege of Delhi lasted roughly from the 1st of July to the 31st of August. However, the encirclement was hardly complete—the rebels could easily receive resources and reinforcements. Later the British were joined by the Punjab Movable Column of Sikh and Pathan soldiers under John Nicholson and elements of the Gurkha Brigade.

Eagerly-awaited heavy siege guns did not guarantee an easy victory against the numerical superiority of the sepoys. Eventually the British broke through the Kashmiri gate and began a week of street fighting. When the British reached the Red Fort, Bahadur Shah had already fled to Humayun's tomb. The British had retaken the city.

The troops of the besieging force proceeded to loot and pillage the city. A large number of the citizens were slaughtered in retaliation for the Europeans and Indian 'collaborators' that had been killed by the rebel sepoys. Artillery was set up in the main mosque in the city and the neighborhoods within the range of artillery were bombarded. These included the homes of the Muslim nobility from all over India, and contained innumerable cultural, artistic, literary and monetary riches. An example would be the loss of most of the works of Mirza Asadullah Khan Ghalib, thought of as the greatest Indian poet of that era.

The British soon arrested Bahadur Shah, and the next day British officer William Hodson shot his sons Mirza Mughal, Mirza Khizr Sultan, and Mirza Abu Bakr under his own authority at the Khooni Darwaza (the bloody gate) near Delhi Gate. Their heads were reportedly presented to their father the next day.

Cawnpore (Kanpur)

In June, sepoys under General Wheeler in Kanpur, (known as Cawnpore by the British) rebelled and besieged the European entrenchment. The British lasted three weeks of the Siege of Cawnpore with little water or food, suffering continuous casualties to men, women and children. On June 25 the Nana Sahib told British troops to surrender and Wheeler had little choice but to accept. The Nana Sahib promised them safe passage to a secure location but when the British boarded riverboats, firing broke out. Who fired first has remained a matter of debate.

During the march to the boats, loyal sepoys were removed by the mutineers and lynched along with any British officer or soldier that attempted to help them, although these attacks were ignored in an attempt to reach the boats safely. After firing began the boat pilots fled, setting fire to the boats, and the rebellious sepoys opened fire on the British, soldiers and civilians. One boat with over a dozen wounded men initially escaped, however, this boat later grounded, was caught by mutineers and pushed back down the river towards carnage at Cawnpore. The female occupants were removed and taken away as hostages and the men, including the wounded and elderly, were hastily put against a wall and shot. Only four men eventually escaped alive from Cawnpore on one of the boats: two privates (both of whom died later during the mutiny), a Lieutenant, and Captain Mowbray Thomson, who wrote a firsthand account of his experiences entitled *The Story of Cawnpore* (London) 1859.

The surviving women and children of the firing were led to Bibi-Ghar (the House of the Ladies) in Cawnpore. On the 15th of July, after noticing the approach of the British forces and believing that they would not advance if there were no hostages to save, their murders were ordered. After the sepoys refused to carry out this order, four butchers from the local market went into the Bibi-Ghar where they proceeded to hack the hostages apart with cleavers and hatchets. The victims' bodies, some still living, were thrown down a well.

The killing of the women and children proved to be a mistake. The British public was aghast and the pro-Indian proponents lost all their support. Cawnpore became a war cry for the British and their allies for the rest of the conflict. The Nana Sahib disappeared and was never heard of again.

When the British retook Cawnpore later, the soldiers took their sepoy prisoners to the Bibi-Ghar and forced them to lick the bloodstains from the walls and floor. They then hanged or "blew from the cannon" the majority of the sepoy prisoners. Although some claimed the sepoys took no actual part in the killings themselves, they did not act to stop it and this was acknowledged by Captain Thompson after the British departed Cawnpore for a second time.

Lucknow

Rebellion erupted in the state of Awadh (also known as Oudh, in modern-day Uttar Pradesh) very soon after the events in Meerut. The British commander of Lucknow, Henry

Lawrence, had enough time to fortify his position inside the Residency compound. British forces numbered some 1700 men, including loyal sepoys. The rebels initial assaults were unsuccessful, and so they began a barrage of artillery and musket fire into the compound. Lawrence was one of the first casualties. The rebels tried to breach the walls with explosives and bypass them via underground tunnels that led to under ground close combat. After 90 days of siege, numbers of British were reduced to 300 loyal sepoys, 350 British soldiers and 550 non-combatants. This action quickly became known as the Siege of Lucknow.

On the September 25 a relief column under the command of Sir Henry Havelock and accompanied by Sir James Outram (who in theory was his superior) fought its way to Lucknow in a brief but well commanded campaign in which the numerically small column defeated mutineer forces in a series of increasingly large battles. This became known as 'The First Relief of Lucknow', as this force was not strong enough to break the siege or extricate themselves and so was forced to join the garrison. In October another, larger, army under the new Commander-in-Chief, Sir Colin Campbell, was finally able to relieve the garrison and on the 18th of November they evacuated the city, the compound women and children leaving first. They then conducted an orderly withdrawal to now-retaken Cawnpore.

Jhansi

Jhansi was a Maratha-ruled princely state in Bundelkhand. When the Raja of Jhansi died without a male heir in 1853, Jhansi was annexed to the British Raj by the Governor-General of India under the Doctrine of Lapse. His widow, Rani Lakshmi Bai, protested the annexation on the grounds that she had not been allowed to adopt a successor, as per Indian custom.

When the Rebellion broke out, Jhansi quickly became a centre of the rebellion. A small group of British officials and their families took refuge in Jhansi's fort, and the Rani negotiated their evacuation. When the British left the fort, they were massacred by the rebels. Although the massacre might have occurred without the Rani's consent, the British suspected her of complicity in the slaughter, despite her protestations of innocence.

In September and October 1857, the Rani led the successful defence of Jhansi from the invading armies of the neighboring rajas of Datia and Orchha. In March 1858, the Central India Field Force, led by Sir Hugh Rose, advanced on and laid siege to Jhansi. The British captured the city, but the Rani fled in disguise.

These events, with significant fictional embellishments, form the basis of John Masters' book, *Nightrunners of Bengal.*

Other Areas

On June 1, 1858, Rani Lakshmi Bai and a group of Maratha rebels captured the fortress city of Gwalior from the Scindia rulers, who were British allies. The Rani was killed three weeks later at the start of the British assault, when she was hit by a spray of bullets after fleeing Gwalior. The British captured Gwalior three days later.

The Rohillas centered in Bareilly were also very active in the war and this area was amongst the last to be captured by the rebels.

Retaliation – "The Devil's Wind"

From the end of 1857, the British had begun to gain ground again. Lucknow was retaken in March 1858. On July 8, 1858, a peace treaty was signed and the war ended. The last rebels were defeated in Gwalior on June 20, 1858. By 1859, rebel leaders Bakht Khan and Nana Sahib had either been slain or had fled. The British adopted the old Mughal punishment for mutiny and sentenced rebels were lashed to the mouth of cannons and blown to pieces. It was a crude and brutal war, with both sides resorting to what would now be described as war crimes. In the end, however, in terms of sheer numbers, the casualties were significantly higher on the Indian side. A letter published after the fall of Delhi in the *"Bombay Telegraph"* and subsequently reproduced in the British press testified to the scale of the retaliation:

".... All the city people found within the walls (of the city of Delhi) when our troops entered were bayoneted on the spot, and the number was considerable, as you may suppose, when I tell you that in some houses forty and fifty people were hiding. These were not mutineers but residents of the city, who trusted to our well-known mild rule for pardon. I am glad to say they were disappointed."

Another brief letter from General Montgomery to Captain Hodson, the conqueror of Delhi exposes how the British military high command approved of the cold blooded massacre of Delhites: "All honor to you for catching the king and slaying his sons. I hope you will bag many more!"

Another comment to the conduct of the British soldiers after the fall of Delhi is of Captain Hodson himself in his book, *Twelve years in India*: "With all my love for the army, I must confess, the conduct of professed Christians, on this occasion, was one of the most humiliating facts connected with the siege."

Edward Vibart, a 19-year-old officer, also recorded his experience: "It was literally murder.... I have seen many bloody and awful sights lately but such a one as I witnessed yesterday I pray I never see again. The women were all spared but their screams on seeing their husbands and sons butchered, were most painful.... Heaven knows I feel no pity, but when some old gray bearded man is brought and shot before your very eyes, hard must be that man's heart I think who can look on with indifference...."

As a result, the end of the war was followed by the execution of a vast majority of combatants from the Indian side as well as large numbers of civilians perceived to be sympathetic to the rebel cause. The British press and British government did not advocate clemency of any kind, though Governor General Canning tried to be sympathetic to native sensibilities, earning the scornful sobriquet "Clemency Canning." Soldiers took very few prisoners and often executed them later. Whole villages were wiped out for apparent pro-rebel sympathies. The Indians called this retaliation "the Devil's Wind."

Reorganization

The rebellion also saw the end of the British East India Company's rule in India. In August, by the Queen's Proclamation of 1858, power was transferred to the British Crown. A secretary of state was entrusted with the authority of Indian affairs and the Crown's viceroy in India was to be the chief executive. The British embarked on a program of reform, trying to integrate Indian higher castes and rulers into the government and abolishing the East India Company.

Militarily, the rebellion transformed both the 'native' and European armies of British India. The British also increased the number of British soldiers in relation to native ones. Regiments which had remained loyal to the British were retained, and Gurkha units, which had been crucial in the Delhi campaign, were increased. The inefficiencies of the old organization, which had estranged sepoys from their British officers, were addressed, and the post-1857 units were mainly organized on the 'irregular' system. Sepoy artillery was abolished also, leaving all artillery in British hands. The post-rebellion changes formed the basis of the military organization of British India until the early twentieth century.

The East India Company's European forces in the three presidency armies (of Bengal, Madras and Bombay) were transferred to the Queen's army. This move precipitated the 'white mutiny' of 1859. European troops, who had enlisted for the Company's army and hoped to secure a bounty for re-engagement with the British army or simply to go home, reacted strongly to the change. European troops in Bengal mounted the largest collective protest the British army has ever seen, forcing the Government of India to offer men their discharge, which over 10,000 accepted. The protest left European military force in India in the hands of the Queen's army.

The viceroy stopped land grabs, decreed religious tolerance and admitted Indians into civil service, albeit mainly as subordinates. Bahadur Shah was tried for treason by a military commission assembled at Delhi, and exiled to Rangoon where he died in 1862, finally bringing the Mughal dynasty to an end. In 1877 Queen Victoria took the title of Empress of India on the advice of her Prime Minister, Benjamin Disraeli. An official report by Sir William W. Hunter (1840-1900) on whether Muslims could be expected to give loyal service to the Queen concluded that they could not be expected to do so but were bound by their faith to rebel. This impacted on how Muslims were treated in British India.

Debate Over Name of Conflict

There is no agreed name for the events of this period, but terms in use include *First War of Independence, War of Independence of 1857, Indian Mutiny* (historically the usual term in British discourse), the *Great Indian Mutiny,* the *Sepoy Mutiny,* the *Sepoy Rebellion,* the *Great Mutiny,* the *Rebellion of 1857* and the *Revolt of 1857.* William Dalrymple, in *The Last Mughal* (2007), refers to it as *the Uprising.* Although many Indian historians do term it as mutiny as well, on the Indian subcontinent it is commonly referred to as a war of independence, and the use of the term *Indian Mutiny* is considered unacceptable and offensive by many, as it is perceived to belittle what they see as a *First War of Independence* and therefore reflecting a biased, imperialistic attitude of the erstwhile colonists.

For example, in October, 2006, the Speaker of the Lok Sabha, the lower house of Indian Parliament said: The War of 1857 was undoubtedly an epoch-making event in India's struggle for freedom. For what the British sought to deride as a mere sepoy mutiny was India's First War of Independence in a very true sense, when people from all walks of life, irrespective of their caste, creed, religion and language, rose against the British rule.

Not only did these martyrs give up their lives for the sake of the country's freedom but also left a message for the future generations — a message of sacrifice, courage of conviction, a strong belief in the ultimate victory of the people in their war against oppression.

With these words, I once again pay my humble tributes to the martyrs of the 1857 War of Independence... Somnath Chaterjee, Office of the Speaker of the Lok Sabha.

Besides this, a contemporary British chronicler, Thomas Lowe, in Central India during the rebellion, wrote in 1860: "To live in India, now, was like standing on the verge of a volcanic crater, the sides of which were fast crumbling away from our feet, while the boiling lava was ready to erupt and consume us." Further, Lowe exclaimed: "The infanticide Rajput, the bigoted Brahmin, the fanatic Mussalman, had joined together in the cause; cow-killer and the cow-worshiper, the pig-hater and the pig-eater... had revolted together."

The government of India celebrated 2007 as the 150th anniversary of "India's First War of Independence."

Debate over the National Character of the Rebellion

Historians remain divided on whether the rebellion can properly be considered a war of Indian independence or not, although it is popularly considered to be one in India. Arguments against include:

- A united India did not exist at that time in political terms;
- The rebellion remained confined to the ranks of the Bengal Army (which nonetheless was the largest of the armies

in India) and in North-Central India;

- The mutiny was put down with the help of other Indian soldiers drawn from the Madras Army, the Bombay Army and the Sikh regiments;
- Many princes and maharajahs did not participate in the rebellion, and those that did were basically interested in reviving and reclaiming their own principalities and fiefdoms, not in creating a United India;
- The Army and the Princes, who were the principal instigators of the rebellion of 1857, played no part in the Nationalist movement as it emerged in the 1880s;
- The Westernized intellectuals supported the British; however, an exception to this rule was Azimullah Khan, a Westernized rebel supporter.

A second school of thought while acknowledging the validity of the above-mentioned arguments opines that this rebellion may indeed be called a war of India's independence. The reasons advanced are:

- Even though the rebellion had various causes (e.g., sepoy grievances, British high-handedness, the Doctrine of Lapse etc.), most of the rebel sepoys set out to revive the old Mughal Empire, that signified a national symbol for them, instead of heading home or joining services of their regional principalities, which would not have been unreasonable if their revolt were only inspired by grievances;
- There was a widespread popular revolt in many areas such as Awadh, Bundelkhand and Rohilkhand. The rebellion was therefore more than just a military mutiny, and it spanned more than one region;
- The sepoys did not seek to revive small kingdoms in their regions, instead they repeatedly proclaimed a "country-wide rule" of the Moghuls and vowed to drive out the British from "India," as they knew it then. (The

sepoys ignored local princes and proclaimed in cities they took over: Khalq Khuda Ki, Mulk Badshah Ka, Hukm Subahdar Sipahi Bahadur Ka - i.e., the world belongs to God, the country to the Emperor and executive powers to the Sepoy Commandant in the city). The objective of driving out "foreigners" from not only one's own area but from their conception of the entirety of "India," signifies a nationalist sentiment;

- The troops of the Bengal Army were used extensively in warfare by the British and had therefore traveled extensively across the Indian subcontinent, leading them perhaps to develop some notion of a nation-state called India. They displayed for the first time in this mutiny, some contemporary British accounts (Malleson) suggest, patriotic sentiments in the modern sense.

In short, we may summarize the discussion in following terms.

1. If the criterion of a National War of Independence is set as "a war (or numerous conflicts) spread all over the nation cutting across regional lines," the rebellion in that case does not qualify as a war of India's independence.
2. If the criterion for a National War of Independence is set as "a war, which even if geographically confined to certain regions, is waged with the intention of driving out from the complete national area a power perceived to be foreign," then it was a war of national independence.

This discussion shows that the term "national war" is subject to individual opinions and cannot be answered decisively.

5

The Indian Mutiny : 1857-1858

One hundred and fifty years after the events of 1857, there is still great debate in what they should actually be called. The British authorities firmly regarded the event as a mutiny by large sections of the Bengal army. Indeed the British were fortunate that it was only the Bengal Army, with a few exceptions, the Bombay and Madras armies stayed remarkably quiescent. The British recognised that there were a number of fellow travellers who joined in and took advantage of the collapse of authority throughout Northern India, notably Ghazis and Gujars.

Post 1947 Indian Nationalists have thought to refer to the events as India's First Nationalist Uprising. It is clear why they would like to brand this event as a nationalist uprising. It was unusual in that it did attract Muslims and Hindus to the cause, but the event was clearly confined to Northern India in general and Bengal in particular.

The truth was obviously somewhere in between. Undoubtedly, the Bengal Army took the lead through their initial mutinies, but they quickly tried to politicise and widen the event through asking the last Mughal Emperor to reassert his claims and reestablish the old Mughal Empire. This did attract wider support but the old Emperor did not have the energy or the resources to fully take on the power of the British in India. The hoped for general Indian uprising never did take place and despite attempts to escalate the events through various atrocities and sieges, the British were able to reorganise their forces in the Indian sub-continent and slowly but surely reestablish their control over the Bengal and other affected areas. Therefore, you could claim to call these events a mutiny that escalated into a rebellion but it never did hit the hoped for nationalist uprising status. For the sake of convenience and familiarity, I will use the term mutiny throughout although with the understanding that it did escalate further.

Causes

Again, there is much debate into why the mutiny did break out in India in 1857. For generations, British schoolboys and girls were told that it all had to do with a misunderstanding and mistakes over a new kind of cartridge issued to the Sepoys and Sowars. Indians were told that 1857 was the 100th anniversary of the Battle of Plassey and that British rule would come to an end on that date. These events certainly did occur and were significant in their own right. However the causes of the mutiny were far more varied and interconnected with one another in quite unforeseen and complicated manners.

Religion

The common thread that will tie most of the factors together and bringing an unlikely alliance between the Muslims and Hindus was the perceived threat to the native religions of the Indian sub-continent. The threat was the increased religious overtones of the East India Company and of the Europeans operating in the sub-continent.

In the eighteenth century, the East India Company had

been interested only in profit and commercial areas. As the nineteenth century progressed, religion began to play a more important role. Consequently, East India personnel took more interest in religious affairs and allowed more missionary work to be carried out under their aegis. This increased religiousity did not make much of a direct impact in terms of converts, but it was certainly noticed by a growing percentage of the Indian population and definitely by the East India Company's employees the sowars and sepoys. Indeed, more and more EIC officers were making unsubtle attempts to expose their soldiers to Christian teachings.

Losing Touch

In fact, the East India Company Officers had had a good reputation for mucking in with their soldiers and were known to lead from the front. In the eighteenth century, EIC officers had been real swashbucklers keen to make their fortune at whatever personal cost. They frequently underwent the same privations and dangers as their charges did. This earned the respect and awe of many Indian company soldiers. As time went on, newer generations of EIC officers were not so hungry for success. There were more British officers for starters and so it was easy for them to stay within the company of like minded officers rather than with their soldiers whose needs and wants they increasingly saw as foreign and peculiar. The officers' language skills consequently suffered which further took them out of the loop of understanding. When families started joining the officers, the break down in contact was almost complete. Officers were having to rely on their Indian NCOs who were very often as aggreived as the soldiers themselves.

Over-Confidence of EIC

Hand in hand with the loss of touch was the over confidence of the East India Company officials. They had become dangerously complacent about their own invincibility. Winning countless small battles at incredible odds had made the EIC seem impregnable. The fact that they were often using far better technology and were better organised only seemed to confirm their right to rule the sub-continent. Over the past century, the EIC had got side-tracked from making money from the ports of Calcutta and Bombay by supplying exotic goods to the people of Britain and the rest of the Empire. In fact scandal and corruption had already converted the East India Company from a trading company to a provider of government services. Ostensibly, this had been done to stamp out corruption and end the monopoly of the EIC over supplying goods. Actually, it would have the long term effect of changing the dynamics of EIC income. Their income would now come from direct taxation. The only ways to increase income was to increase taxation or to rule over an expanded empire. Neither of these methods would be popular with the Indian population. Whilst the company was making itself more unpopular in the areas it controlled, it would soon find that its armies were tied down in the newly conquered areas and their borders. The ratio of Europeans to Indians in the armed forces in the existing Indian Empire was reaching perilously low levels.

Dalhousie's Reforms

In 1848, James Ramsay, the Earl of Dalhousie, became Governor General of India. It was thought that he would represent a steadying influence on the colony and would control its budget. Dalhousie though attempted to spur on the modernisation and Europeanisation of the Colony. A department of Public Works was set up; telegraphs, railways, ports were all to be built or to be upgraded. The Ganges canal was to irrigate huge swathes of central India. Metalled roads were to be built. A postal system was set up. New engineering colleges were set up. Promotion was to be on merit rather than seniority. Tea plantations were encouraged and provided with the infrastructure to take away their products. He encouraged Christian missionaries and societies to provide missions to care for the needy and low caste Indians. These reforms, and many more, were intended to improve the efficiency of colony in the long run. The short term investment costs though would prove unpalatable and put yet more strain on the taxation system. He would also preside over the resurrection and implementation of the infamous 'doctrine of lapse' which will be expanded upon below. He retired due to ill health in 1856 - just before the mutiny - and was expecting a heroes welcome for his reforms but instead found himself having to defend himself against the charges of having stirred up the socio-economic structure of India to beyond breaking point.

Technology

EIC soldiers and other Indians would view many of the technological changes with trepidation. Steam trains and steam ships seemed to be some ungodly creature that defied the laws of nature. The new communications systems threatened many existing castes and businesses. Boatmen would be put out of the haulage business, farmers would find their local monopolies being challenged by cheaper imports from elsewhere in India or even further afield. Mass produced British made goods could be imported far more cheaply and efficiently than the locals could produce themselves. Severe strains were being placed on the existing economic systems by the very tools that were supposed to make India more efficient. Soldiers would have the added complication of new equipment and tactics to adapt to. With the expansion of the Indian Empire, soldiers were travelling further and further from their homes. Expeditions in Burma, the Middle East and further afield also required soldiers to travel over water. For high born Brahmins, this meant the loss of their caste. Technological change brought as many fears as benefits to the Indians in the 1850s.

The Doctrine of Lapse

Simply put, the doctrine of lapse allowed the company to

annex the principality of any Indian ruler who died without natural heirs or one who was manifestly incompetent. It was thought that this would be a fairly painless way for the company to expand its Indian Empire (and therefore its tax base) by avoiding any direct confrontations or military annexations. It was hoped that the Indians did not really mind who their rulers were and would fatalistically live with the changes far above their heads. It was hoped that they would appreciate British efficiency and incorruptability. Satara was the first state to be annexed this way, Jaitpur, Sambalpur, Nagpur and Jhansi would follow suit. The practice of Indian princes adopting heirs was conveniently placed aside by Dalhousie. In 1856 the EIC would pick up the richest of the states in this manner. It was declared that the Oudh was being mismanaged by its incompetent ruler and so was annexed. Oudh was a very rich and probably corrupt Indian state but it was one that was understood and appreciated by its population. The British were thought of as inflexible and alien. It was also not appreciated just how large a proportion of the EIC sepoy army came from Oudh. They had been happy to take the King's shilling as any mercenary would, but many of them were horrified to find that their own homes had been annexed in such an underhand and unfair way.

Overstretch

The decade before the mutiny had been a busy decade for both the British and EIC armies. The British army had just been involved in the hugely complicated and disastrously run Crimean campaign from 1854 to 1856. Apart from the manpower costs of this campaign, it was hardly an advertisement to the world on the efficiency of the British Army. Many observers felt that the British might be a paper tiger after all. Azimullah Khan who would later advise the infamous Nana Sahib was just one such observer. He felt that the Turks or the Russians might provide better long term allies for the Indians. The EIC armies had been busy in 1848/

9 in the annexation of Punjab and Sindh with the Anglo-Sikh Wars. There had been war in Burma and many smaller scale battles along the frontiers. The Santal Expedition had shown how even poorly equipped peasant armies could cause huge logistical problems for the EIC army. On top of all this was the stationing of the EIC armies in the newly acquired lands. This policy was thought prudent lest the newly acquired peoples rose up against their new masters. The EIC assumed that those areas it had ruled for decades or more were firmly under their control.

Cartridges

The infamous cartridge difficulties combined religious sensibilities with technological change. For years the EIC had relied on a simple but inaccurate smooth bore musket. It was decided to introduce a more accurate muzzle loading Enfield Rifled Musket. One way to speed up the loading process was the introduction of a paper cartridge with the bullet sitting on the exact quantity of powder needed. The loader was required to bite open this paper cartridge to expose the powder. The original cartridges were made in Britain and had been covered in tallow to help protect the cartridge from the elements. Unfortunately the tallow had been made from a beef and pork fat. To the British users of these cartridges, this made no big deal. Hindu and Muslim users were horrified at the defiling fat. The EIC quickly realised its blunder and replaced the animal fat with vegetable fat but the damage had already been done. To Hindus and Muslims alike, their worst fears of being ritually humiliated had been confirmed. Many assumed that this had been a deliberate policy by the Europeans who were looking to impose their own religion on the sub-continent. Battalion after battalion refused to use the new cartridges. Some even refused to handle the cartridges when officers had allowed them the option of tearing open the cartridges instead of biting them. As far as the officers were concerned, refusing to obey an order was tantamount to mutiny as it was. Different commanders handled the situation in different ways - some with more sensitivity than others. The first shots were to be fired by (an inebriated) Mangal Pandey on March 29th at Barrackpore. He protested against the disbanding of a unit that had disobeyed orders to use the cartridges. He shot at a British sergeant-major and a lieutenant and then engaged them in a sword fight. He saw the two of them off but then shot himself in the chest when General Hearsey arrived in the parade ground. The authorities at Barrackpore were forutunate to have the European 84th regiment to hand so that the disarming of the Indian battalions could be done with the threat of force for any sepoys thinking of refusing to hand over their guns. Not all stations would be so fortunate.

Reforms of Dalhousie and the Sepoy Uprising (1848–1858)

The mid nineteenth century India, under the British rule, experienced monumental changes in both its socio-economic and political scenes that laid the foundation for the Indian National Movement, which became the precursor to the eventual ouster of the British rule and establishment of an independent India. Ninety years before gaining independence from the British by peaceful means-largely due to the tenacity and perseverance of one man, Gandhi – the concerted effort to remove the British had begun by an armed and bloody revolt by the Indian soldiers serving under the British army.

This event of 1857-58 came to be known as the Sepoy Mutiny-implying a failed attempt by armed thugs who were biting the hands of the legitimate overlords that fed them (the term Sepoy-originally *Sipahi* – referred to soldiers of Indian origin who served in the British armed forces). However, the uprising was more a revolt than a mere mutiny against the British. The British had found great success with little bloodshed in amassing substantial acreage of land in India, and were busy with implementation of 'reforms' in order to civilize the 'barbaric natives' at an accelerated pace. The decade between 1848 and 1858 was an event filled one that altered the course of the British history in India.

Hindu widows were allowed to remarry, by decree. Earlier in the century *sati* (the practice of immolation of the wife in the funeral pyre of her dead husband) and *thugi* (ritual murder by strangling and highway robbery in the service of Mother Goddess Kali) had both been abolished by William Bentinck with the assistance of Rajaram Mohan Roy. The princely states, which thus far had been loyal allies of the British, were systematically stripped of their privileged domains, and their lands were annexed under the pretext of "lapse" and "paramountcy." The treaties between princely states and the John Company were ignored especially if there was no natural "heir and successor."

The long standing Hindu practice of adopting a son to succeed the throne, if no natural male heir was available was outlawed with the stroke of a pen and old treaties were torn apart. If the land belonging to princely states could not be acquired by this means, other excuses were invented such as depravity of citizens and inept administration by the princes etc. Another wily tact was also followed when the pensioner's titles and pensions awarded to princes and other land owners as compensation for lands seized from them were also allowed to "lapse" and not renewed.

Dalhousie's Reforms

James Andrew Broun Ramsay, Marquee of Dalhousie (1812 – 1860) had been appointed the governor-general of India by the Company in 1848. He was on a mission to unify India and control it. He earnestly believed that more of India annexed by the British the better it was for the Indians. First order of business was to let the internal feud in Punjab fester and then wage war with the ruler at Lahore. The master mind of Punjabi Empire, Ranjit Singh had died leaving behind weak replacements. After subduing the Sikh army, Dalhousie quickly annexed their lands, including Kashmir that was under their rule. Kashmir was then sold to Gulab Singh, who once was a feudatory of the mighty Ranjit Singh. The kingdom of Kashmir would enjoy relative independence until the next one hundred years and the progeny of Gulab Singh. Only after the Indian independence, would Hari Singh, the last maharaja of Kashmir aligned himself with India, which in turn set the stage for the struggle in Kashmir that even rages today.

Dalhousie started his cunning annexations in the year 1848 and the social reforms were shoved down the throats of Indians. Both Hindu and Muslim orthodoxy had always been viewed as barbaric, and social reforms were passed as laws with little sensitivity towards ancient religious practices of both Hindus and Muslims. It had also not gone unnoticed by the Hindus and Muslims that a slew of missionaries had appeared in India in the early part of 19th century. Conversions of Hindus were carried on without much objection, though there was much discomfiture among the orthodox Hindus. Moreover, a large contingent of young British men eagerly coveted positions in the company, solely for the purpose of infusing "civilization" to the misdirected "heathen natives." By mid century full blown discrimination was practiced by giving preference in civil jobs and other monetary rewards to those who converted to Christianity.

Dalhousie and the company were basking in glory in the aftermath of their success in Punjab, which was now firmly under the control of British after the treaty with the Sikhs. Revenues from the fertile soil of Punjab had exceeded their wildest dreams. The company stockholders in London were very pleased. The English language had been chosen as the language in schools and colleges over few objections. Sanskrit and other common native languages had been relegated to secondary and minority status. This had created a class of Indian intelligentsia which was vying for education in the English language both at home and abroad in England. A new class of Indians was developing that was in little touch with native languages and cultures and consider themselves more English than Indian.

Dalhousie did not confine himself to social reforms. He had visions of unifying the entire country through railroad. His goal was to connect the major British residencies in Madras, Bombay and Calcutta by rail. Construction began in 1850. The first was built in Calcutta, a 150 mile long railroad track connecting Howrah (opposite Calcutta on the right bank of River Hughly) to the coal mines of Raniganj.

Another was built in Bombay, a shorter route of only 21 miles between Bombay and Thana. Dalhousie considered railways to be the greatest boon to India ever conferred by England. Two other modes of communication were also considered equally important by Dalhousie in modernizing India. Telegraph and postal services throughout India were both started under his watch. First telegraph lines were laid in 1851 by the brilliant and ingenious Dr. William O'Shaughnessey in Bengal. Soon work was begun to connect Madras, Calcutta, Agra, Lahore and Bombay by wire. As the construction of thousand mile links were completed in 1854, Dalhousie took personal pleasure in receiving telegraphic messages from O'Shaughnessey. 2500 miles of telegraphic wires had been laid out in a single year in 1854.

India's first Post Office Act had been enacted in 1837 but the completion of telegraphic links gave an additional impetus to it. Dalhousie again took personal interest in modernizing the inefficient postal system and soon the half-anna letter was able to reach many remote corners of India. Within three months of its implementation, the number of letters delivered by the postal service increased by 50 percent. Communication within the country was revolutionized. One-anna newspapers, a uniform price throughout the country increased the opinion making potential at all levels. What Dalhousie had explicitly pronounced in his summary minutes to the directors of the company on the eve of his departure to India had come to fruition. "Three great engines of social improvement, which the sagacity and science of recent times had previously given to the Western nations – I mean Railways, uniform Postage and the Electric Telegraph," he had said would harness India's bullock-cart civilization. In short, Dalhousie had succeeded in implementing sweeping reforms in India in an attempt to create a Europe-like society in a single decade in the mid 19th century.

Dalhousie's plan for modernizing and unifying the country was indeed a selfish one. The railways could speed the process of exporting raw materials to Manchester textile mills. Swift transportation of the military to potentially troubled spots was another reason. After all, a country with a population of 200 million was being controlled by a mere 40,000 strong British troops with 232,000 Sepoys under their command. With all the annexations the country was getting too large to be safely administered without the tools of modern communication and transportation. Any miscue on the administration's part could result in quick riot and revolt that could not be contained by the minority British rulers.

This was the same reason he pushed for the expensive proposal to implement telegraphic links. Dalhousie was not prescient of the upcoming mutiny of 1857 but nevertheless, his plan of connecting the country through telegraphic wires might have saved the British Empire in India, as the news was swiftly transmitted to other areas before trouble began. In some areas, preemptive actions were taken by the British that prevented the mutineers from inflicting more damage.

The railways had been a huge success with the general population. Travel by train increased by leaps and bounds. The improved communication and transportation also connected Indians in many ways. Soon a nationalistic movement would be born but the triad of Dalhousie's ventures was not the sole cause for adding fuel to the fire that was burning among the Sepoys. It was more because of the social reforms that had been enacted at breakneck speed which threatened the very core of the existence of orthodox Hindu and Muslim societies.

Hindu and Muslim Discontentment

Dalhousie annexed Oudh with ease in February of 1856 under some pretext and complaint about the corrupt and capricious king of Oudh being not fit to rule. King Wajid Ali handed over his kingdom without any armed resistance. He petitioned Dalhousie in Calcutta, who by now was totally disinterested. Wajid Ali then travelled to London to appeal to the British authorities, but only succeeded in addressing stone faced men who were not interested in hearing his cause. He returned to India and started a conspiracy with the Brahmins and Kshatriya soldiers of Oudh, who had formed the backbone of the Sepoy Army of Bengal.

The straw that broke the camel's back was when the British introduced modern weaponry of breech-loading Enfield rifles to the army. New cartridges were greased with animal fat and lard and the soldier had to bite off the tip before loading it on to the rifle. Rumours of cattle and pig fat being used in the cartridges spread slowly and the British had paid little attention to the complaints.

This was sacrilegious for Hindus who considered cows as sacred, and for Muslims handling of pigs had been considered irreligious. The "barbarians" with their archaic practices did not deserve to be heard, and sensitive matters of religious taboos were completely ignored. Soldiers who refused to load the rifles with cartridges tainted with animal fat were summarily dismissed and shamefully made to walk home without pay or pension.

Dalhousie had returned to England in 1856, a lonely and sick man, and Lord Charles James Canning was the new governor – general. Canning had enacted several unpopular measures when he took office.

Most distressing was a new law called the General Services Act that forced Sepoys to be deployed away from homeland, especially to Burma. This Act alone had produced dissatisfaction among the soldiers. Brahmins and other high caste Hindus considered it pollution if made to cross the "dark waters." Dalhousie had already enacted the Caste Disabilities Act of 1850 that permitted converts to Christianity to inherit property. This had appeared as a concerted Christian conspiracy to shake the foundations of the Hindu orthodoxy. In 1856 another law allowing Hindu widows to remarry was passed by Canning that added more discord among Hindus. Sati had already been banned since 1829, and this additional meddling into Hindu customs was not welcomed in high caste Hindu society.

Rumours started by the conspirators about dead pigs in the water supply and ground cow bones in sugar added more fuel to the anger of Sepoys. A quiet recruitment, especially by people loyal to Wajid Ali and Peshwa Nana Sahib of the Marathas, went on for the first five months of 1857. Members of Bahadur Shah's (the last Mughal Emperor in Delhi) court and Dost Muhammad's agents from Kabul were also silently recruited. For five months the Sepoys organized quietly, with the aid of disgruntled monarchies which had been either dethroned or marginalized by the British.

The Sepoy Uprising

On Saturday May 9, 1857 eighty-five Sepoys were shackled and marched to prison in Meerut because they refused to load their Enfield rifles with cartridges tainted with lard. The other Sepoys silently watched the spectacle but this event served as the battle cry for the revolt. Next morning, which was on Sunday, armed Sepoys marched against their British superiors. Most of them were dragged out of churches and killed.

The prisoners were released and the frenzied mob marched thirty miles south to Delhi, shouting "Chalo Dilli" ("Let's go to Delhi"). The Mughal king Bahadur Shah II was a reluctant accomplice as he had grown old in his throne. However the revolutionists elevated him to "Emperor of India" status, and with little resistance from the British in Delhi, declared it "liberated" on May 11.

Soon the entire Ganges belt, the heartland of Hindustan, was lost to the British. Oudh (Lucknow) was well defended by chief commissioner Sir Henry Lawrence until he could get reinforcements in November. Kanpur (Kanpur) however was a disaster. Four hundred men, women and children could only hold out for eighteen days but then surrendered to Peshwa Nana Sahib. A deal was struck for safe passage to Allahabad along the river, but when the British families climbed into waiting boats, they were all massacred. This event triggered so much anger among the British that it served as a lightning rod for future atrocities by the British against the Indians, following their regaining control of Indian heartland.

Illustration of the Revolt From London Printing Company Limited

The victors failed to unite among their various factions of Muslims, Marathas and other Hindu soldiers. Moreover, the revolt failed to catch fire in the south. Madras and Bombay were quiet and showed no interest in joining forces with their northern brothers. In addition to Muslim rulers of Oudh and Delhi, local rulers like Devi Singh in Mathura and Kadam Singh of Meerut became heroes of the revolt and rallied the peasants to join in their cause. But only Delhi, Lucknow and Kanpur remained the centres of revolt, which soon lost steam from lack of sustained strategy against the British and lack of cooperation between the mutineers.

The land owners in the countryside were not too enthusiastic about the revolt as they feared losing their lands to new owners and increased burden of taxation. Bickering fights and jealousies among local rajas and nawabs, and the failure of the revolutionists to pacify traditional landowners spelt doom for the sustenance of the revolt.

The Aftermath

British never feared a total loss, especially when the initial fury of the revolt was not maintained. Once widespread revolt was held in check, they just waited for the internal feud among the participants to fester. While they never doubted their ability to gain back control of the Ganges heartland, a fury and vengeance was well under way against the Indians. Men who were known for their patience and balanced approach towards the natives had suddenly turned into raging murderers. Indiscriminate killing of all classes of Indians began as soon as the opportunity arose. Long serving domestic servants of British families were executed under suspicion of seditious activities. Suspects were tied to the cannons and blown away. Live flaying of unsuspecting villagers and peasants was advocated. One hundred years of building bridges of confidence and trust between the British and the Indians were being abandoned only because of unfounded suspicion and innuendo. The print media, while very vocal about the atrocities of the Sepoys in Kanpur and Lucknow, were now silent about the barbaric execution of innocent people without any proof of wrongdoing or any trial.

Near Kanpur, entire villages were burnt and the people killed. Delhi was recaptured by the British, with the help of Sikh regiment by September 20, 1857 and Bahadur Shah II was exiled to Burma. His sons were murdered in cold blood, and the Emperor himself died in 1858 in exile, thus bringing an end to three hundred years of glorious Mughal history in India.

Pockets of resistance from smaller groups went on until summer of 1858. Rani Lakshmibai of Jhansi put up a gallant fight along with Tantia Topi, the artillery expert of Peshwa Nana Sahib. The Rani had lost her kingdom due to the "lapse and paramountcy" of Dalhousie, as she had no male heirs and her adopted son was not recognized as a legal heir. The Rani died fighting on her horse and Tantia Topi was captured and hung along with many other rebels.

The revolution was not as small as the British would have liked to characterize as a mutiny. However, it was much smaller than an independence struggle, as the Indians would like to call it. But it did bring about monumental changes in India.

It proved to be the nail on the coffin of the Mughal Empire, independent Oudh and the rule of the Maratha Peshwas. There was discontent in Britain about so many British citizens losing their lives and above all the whole episode of Sepoy uprising costing so much revenue to control it.

It had cost England a full year's worth of Indian revenue- 36 million pounds. A debate ensued whether Dalhousie's zeal for accelerated pace of reforms or the antiquated administration of the company were to be blamed for the unfortunate turn of events. The company was the scapegoat and the administration of India came into the hands of British Crown, under Queen Victoria.

In August 1858, the British Parliament passed the Government of India Act, transferring all rights that the company had over India to the British Crown, thus effectively ending the rule of the Company Raj, which had lasted one hundred years since the Battle of Plassey, when Robert Clive defeated Siraj-ud-daula, the nawab of Bengal on June 23, 1757. Last governor-general of the company, Lord Canning, stayed on as the first viceroy of India ruled by the British Crown.

Military Aspect

The company's native army had performed very well for over a century winning large part of India for the company and bringing stability. Company's army was not a static entity but a self-sustained living cosmos which was itself undergoing a significant change. The usual ripples accompanied with these changes were also occurring whether someone was noticing it or not at that time. Overall, there has been a gradual change in the Company's army. The native army which conquered India for the John Company was composed of autonomous regiments. The British officers posted in these regiments were for life. They saw themselves as 'fathers' of the native sepoys. The 'commanders could reward or punish their sepoys with almost complete impunity'. By 1840s, there were significant changes.

The young officers of the company started to distance themselves from the native sepoys. One factor was the arrival of increasing numbers of European women. Earlier British officers lived with native concubines and even married native women. Most British officers were well versed with native languages, knew the cultures of their regiments and mixed with native officers and sepoys. Now the younger generation of officers, both bachelor and married developed their own little white worlds, increasing the gulf between them and their native sepoys. 'The men were badly treated, sworn at, and called "niggers" and "pigs". The annexation of new territories needed new administrators and several military officers were posted to civilian jobs. Officers coveted these civilian jobs as they brought more money, fame, honour and a break from monotonous garrison life. In early 1850s, Colonel Frederick McKesson was civil commissioner of Peshawar while Lieutenant Harry Lumsden was serving as deputy commissioner and Captain James an assistant commissioner. Similarly many officers like Nixon in Bhurutpur and McPherson in Gwalior were serving at civilian posts. Old and infirm officers were left behind to command the regiments. The centralization and reform decreased the authority of officers of the regiment as the list of regulations kept proliferating. Any measure of extra money for sepoys going on far away campaigns advocated by military officers were fought furiously by company bosses in Calcutta. In July 1856, general enlistment order was proclaimed which stated that sepoy would serve anywhere if ordered. This meant that a Hindu might have to cross the dreaded 'Black Waters' at the cost of losing his caste. In early 1857, rumours were rife among native sepoys in many cantonments. The sepoys of 2nd Bengal Native Infantry (BNI) told their Colonel that there were unmistakable signs that the company was bent on destroying the religion of the natives. They pointed to contamination of salt, ghee and sugar of its sepoys with the bones of pigs and cows. Hindu soldiers interpreted the reddish colour of the salt from the dye of the sack as cow's blood.

A.H. Amin has discussed in some detail the perception of company's military effectives by the native sepoys. We with the benefit of command of different languages and historical hindsight can see these things more clearly but the perception of sepoys in 1857 needs a more careful evaluation. Surely, the setbacks of company's army in late eighteenth and early nineteenth century would have affected the perception of native participants of these battles. The overall impact about half a century later on a new generation of native soldiers, mostly illiterate and with no means of information or communications with other parts of the country would have a limited impact. Even the more recent campaigns against the Sikhs were viewed in the light of overall victory of British arms and sepoys were not in a position to do a critical analysis of the setbacks in individual battles. More important is the fact that the scenes which they witnessed after the start of rebellion had a more pronounced effect on the sepoys. Murder of British officers, refuge of civil and military officers in entrenchments and general breakdown of law and order in affected areas would be a more powerful signal to the wavering native troops that the company's rule was about to end. Having said that, it is also true that at least there was dent in the aura of invincibility of the British arms with defeat in First Afghan War and setbacks against Sikhs. More important than the military setbacks in Afghanistan was the psychological trauma of sepoys. Subedar Hidayat Ali, a third generation of loyal sepoy of the company wrote in 1858 to his British superiors about the troubles of sepoys during Afghanistan campaign. Hindu sepoys were fearful of losing their caste. Their colleagues refused to smoke or dine with them as they were considered outcasts.

Although in later part of rebellion there was general disaffection in most regiments of Bengal army but in the early part of the rebellion, the regiments which started the mutiny in their stations need to be carefully studied. They had particular historical background and specific immediate causes of unrest. Only A.H. Amin has looked into this aspect in some cases. The 3rd Cavalry which started the rebellion in Meerut had run into problems in September 1855 when stationed at Bolarum near Hyderabad.

During Muharram, Colonel Mackenzie had issued a cantonment order of prohibiting noisy procession at midnight. After realizing that it was Muharram, the order was cancelled. The procession in which several cavalrymen participated proceeded along the route and in front of Colonel Mackenzie's house there was a heated conversation between Colonel and some participants of the procession. Later, there was an attempt on Colonel Mackenzie's life. Some cavalrymen later told Colonel Carpenter that they were loyal to the government but their religion has been insulted. In an inquiry all native commissioned officers of 3rd Cavalry were with two exceptions dismissed. The 2nd Native Cavalry stationed at Kanpur had an interesting history.

It was raised in 1787 and had fought bravely in various campaigns. In 1840, two companies of the regiment fled when confronted by a small body of Afghan horsemen. The exact cause was never established. One possibility is the origin of troopers of the regiment which were mainly Afghans of Qandahar origin who had settled in Lucknow and they may not wanted to confront their ethnic kin though separated by a time span of sixty years. The outraged commander disbanded the whole regiment and all European officers were transferred to 11th Native Cavalry. In 1850, one of the old officers captured the Sikh standard in Multan. Impressed by this feat of bravery, the Company restored the old number of 2nd Cavalry. Nana Sahib's commander of the guard, Jawala Prasad worked on the disgruntled Risaldar Teeka Singh and won him and his house in the lines became the centre for all disaffected sowars. The 56th BNI at Banda was involved in operations against Santals in 1855-56.

The operations against Santals were different than earlier campaigns against many local armies. This was a scorched earth policy in which sepoys burned villages and hanged Santals. It was more a counter-insurgency operation rather than the romantic headlong charges on enemy forces.

This gave the sepoys their first encounter in suppressing civilian population on a large scale. The wife of Captain William Halliday of 56th BNI had Bible printed in Urdu and Nagri and distributed among the sepoys convincing them that the British were there to convert them to Christianity. 10th Native Infantry stationed in Fatehgarh which rebelled had officers like Major William Lindsay who had spent most of his career as a staff officer with little interaction with his sepoys. It was commanded by a mediocre sixty years old Lt. Colonel George Smith who had served most of his life in 47th BNI and had taken charge of 10th at Fatehgurh. He had seen his last action in the battlefield about thirty-eight years ago. The sepoys did not know him. His second-in-command was fifty one year old Captain Robert Munro who had managed to serve in the Indian army for thirty years without ever fighting a battle.

The 10th BNI also had a peculiar experience. This regiment had served in Burma travelling in ships. Brahmins called the sea, 'Black Water' and believed that they will lose their caste by crossing the sea. The regiment had agreed when their officers had promised rewards which never came. Locals jeered the regiment as Christian Regiment. The local scene was spiced by the affair of pensioned Nawab with the wife of an ensign Reginald Byrne. The ensign when seeing his wife with Nawab, had kicked him out of the door. The 19th and 34th Bengal Native Infantry were at Lucknow at the time of annexation of Oudh. It was quite natural that sepoys were affected by the general discontent which was aroused with the annexation.

In February 1857 both these regiments were in Barrackpore. When 19th BNI came to know about new cartridges, they refused. The Colonel confronted them angrily with artillery and cavalry on the parade ground but then accepted their demand to withdraw the artillery and cancel next morning parade. On March 29, Mangal Pandey of 34th BNI (the regiment was thoroughly disaffected due to the zealous Christian preaching by its commandant Colonel Wheler) shot at two British but when the General John Hearsey (an officer of old school) came himself thundering on the parade ground alone, Mangal turned his musket to himself and wounded himself in chest. Two days later, when 19th BNI was being disbanded, the sepoys were weeping in front of Hearsey and blessing him for his mercy. Lt. Colonel George Smith who was not popular among the officers and men commanded the 3rd Cavalry which rebelled at Meerut. When the condemned sepoys were marched off to jail, they threw their boots at Lt. Colonel Smith. Quite a contrast to how the disbanded sepoys behaved to General Hearsey.

Several regimental officers who had spent long years with their sepoys trusted fully their native sepoys. Colonel Thomas Pierce of 6th Light Cavalry stationed at Nasirabad sent his eight-month pregnant wife to sleep in the quarters of native officers families. His sowars had a bloody skirmish with the rebellious 15th Bengal Native Infantry. Later they switched sides but didn't harm their officers. Colonel Wart had vowed that if his regiment mutinies it may walk over his body, but he will never leave it. 47th BNI at Mirzapur remained loyal as it was commanded by a wise old Colonel David Pott greatly respected by his men. Colonel George Sherer of 73rd BNI stationed at Jalpaiguri was of the view that disarming native regiments was counterproductive. He never even carried any personal weapon with him while with his troops in line Patrick Grant of Madras Army had avoided the problem of greased cartridges by allowing his soldiers to lubricate their cartridges with Ghee, clarified butter rather than animal fat. 31st BNI at Saugor remained staunchly loyal, without any support from British soldiers, under their own native officers they chased and defeated the mutinous 42nd BNI and captured their colours and arms.

The Ist and 3rd Cavalry and 2nd Infantry were stationed in Aurangabad. These regiments were composed mainly of Muslims. In late June 1857, when the troops came to know that they might be part of the force of General Woodburn to advance on Delhi, there was disaffection among the Ist Cavalry. The prompt arrival of Woodburn, disarming of small number of mutineers and escape of one troop stabilized the situation.

The troops remained loyal to British and 3rd Cavalry under Captain Orr fought well against Holkar's troops. Many native officers like Risaldar Major Bhawani Singh of Ist Cavalry, Jemadar Khoda Buksh of 56th BNI remained loyal even when their regiments mutinied. Sebedar Ram Baksh begged to be allowed to join the garrison at the entrenchment of Cawnpur but was not allowed. He tried to carry the regimental record in a cart to safety but was looted by a band of peasants. 53rd and 56th BNI at Cawnpur were steadfast. They were repeatedly taunted, abused and threatened by the rebel troopers of Ist Cavalry and even then only part of the regiments joined the rebels.

In fact several sepoys of 53rd assembled on parade ground with their arms to help British officer quell the mutiny but by now General Wheeler was not sure himself and he ordered artillery fire on the sepoys thus assuring their desertion. Similarly, in Benaras when native regiments were being disarmed, Ludhiana Regiment (consisting of Sikhs) mistakenly thought that they were also being disarmed and rebelled.

After the uprising at Meerut, the situation for British became very difficult. In fact, the very instrument of disarming of native regiments to prevent the rebellion became the main immediate cause of outright mutiny by native soldiers. The attempts at disarming and dismounting of native regiments caused panic and panic quickly escalated to revolt. Whenever disarming was attempted, the sepoys thought they have lost the confidence of the British and European troops will mow them down without any qualm.

The British officers and men fought with a determination and passion as they were defending their own homeland. This is the reason that even today, it is considered a glorious chapter of British military history. In the later part of rebel operations, as the atrocities on women and children by the rebels were known, revenge became the force multiplier. In many battles of the rebellion, 'interior impulses, largely vindictive, made the British fight with a demonic energy and contempt for the odds which were often stacked against them'. The British won the day due to the presence of dare-devil young officers who led from the front. In several instances brave officers were able to weld the wavering sepoys together and prevent the mutiny.

One such officer was Captain Edmund Vibart of 2nd Native Cavalry. In May 1857, he was passing through Fatehgurh to Nainital. When the riot in prison started, the sepoy guard just watched. Captain Vibart was hit on his face by a brick. The enraged, bleeding Vibart ordered the sepoys to charge on the prison. The sepoys fired, killing several prisoners and chased remaining into their cells. One gallant officer by his action was able to rally wavering sepoys which even didn't belong to his regiment. In Delhi, it was the tenacity of Richard Baird-Smith which prevented the timid General Wilson to retreat from the ridge. Officers like Hodson, Nicholson and Collin Cambell saved the day for the British.

It is very difficult to assess and analyze why in one place the sepoy rebelled while in another place he remained staunchly loyal. What factors influenced him in the critical hour of making that decision of dishonour his oath and colours. One cannot generalize the motives of all the sepoys. The colonel of 47th BNI devised an ingenious plan telling his men to loan their pay to locals at high interest rates. The sepoys wanted no part of any anarchy as they will lose high income. Maharajah Jiyaji Rao Scindia of Gwalior sided with British. He only financed his contingent which consisted of sepoys who were recruited on the pattern of Bengal Army.

The sepoys mutinied on June 14 but never marched to Delhi. While A.H. Amin attributes this to clever propaganda by the Maharajah but more important factor was the fact that Maharajah continued to pay their salaries, so they had a more convincing reason to stay at Gwalior. In the early part of the rebellion, most of the rebel sepoys and their leaders fought bravely and with tenacity. As the sieges prolonged, the inner conflicts emerged and initial euphoria dissipated, the sepoys started to waver. In Delhi, due to the laxity of discipline and avoidance of many sepoys to fight, Bakht Khan issued an order that no man who left in the morning to fight could return within the walls until 4 p.m. He also decreed that no man would qualify for the day's pay until he had done battle with British. Several sepoys quietly left for their homes. 17th BNI at Azamgarh, after mutiny plundered the treasury. When they reached Faizabad, they were relieved of their loot by the rebels from Jaunpur and Benaras. The rebels out of control were a larger threat than the British. The rapid deterioration of discipline among sepoys dismayed many. In Oudh, Subedar Teeka Singh of 2nd Cavalry became general while Jemadar

Durga Singh of 53rd BNI became colonel. His angry Muslim troopers who accused him of amassing private wealth summarily arrested the newly promoted General Teeka Singh. One aspect of the rebellion which has not been studied and discussed in detail is the murder of British officers and their families.

As it is now clear that there was not a large scale general conspiracy to overthrow Company's rule. Most rebellions in garrisons were local affairs prompted by local causes or excitement generated by the news of successes of rebels in other areas. Even in one regiment, there was not a unanimous decision of all sepoys to mutiny. Many sepoys did not condone the behaviour of the rebel comrades but were caught in the eye of the storm. The ringleaders of the rebellion aware of this clear and present danger probably executed officers and their families as a first act to make sure that there was no going back. This act assured that all sepoys who may not be agreeing with the plans of the rebels have now to throw their lot as after the murder of the officers it was clear to everyone that there will be no pardon or mercy.

In several places British officers were shot or cut to pieces on parade grounds or in their homes. Ironically, the same was to be done more than a century later in East Pakistan (now Bangladesh). East Bengal Regiments which mutinied in 1971, took a page from the history of 1857 rebellion. Although there was a general resentment among the Bengali sepoys but it was the action of junior Bengali officer to execute West Pakistani senior officers in front of the sepoys to assure mutiny of the whole regiment. In Jhansi, 12th BNI and 14th Irregular Cavalry was stationed. On June 5, 1857, only one company of 12th led by one native sergeant marched to Star Fort and became rebellious. The remaining four companies of 12th and 14th Cavalry remained loyal and on parade professed their loyalty and were angry at the conduct of rebellious company.

It was after the murder of commander of the troops, Captain Dunlop that the remaining sepoys joined the rebels.

Other officers like Ensign Taylor, Lt. Turnbull and Sergeant Major Newton were killed in the early part of the rebellion. The remaining garrison along with women and children was put to sword by the orders of the Risaldar. Similarly the detachment of 12th BNI at Naogaon commanded by Major Kirk, volunteered to serve against the rebels. A portion of them rebelled after the news of murder of whole garrison of Jhansi arrived in Naogaon.

Only A.H. Amin has discussed in detail the role of Enfield rifle in the conflict and its impact on the results of war. There is no doubt that superior weapons are a key factor in the outcome of wars but the issue has to be evaluated more carefully. In early nineteenth century, the romance of all armies including India army 'lay in its assaults: glorious, audacious, headlong rushes on the enemy' all despite their effectiveness against assault disdained trenches and foxholes. Whenever this technique was used such as by Wheeler's entrenchment in Cawnpur and by rebels in Lucknow, it was successful. Enfield played a significant role but not in all battles of the rebellion. His statement that, 'it was above all the "Enfield" Rifle which was the real victor of 1857'[30] seems to be a very general and we need to look more carefully at the role of Enfield.

The effectiveness of Enfield played a significant role in some battles of the mutiny like the battle of Trimu Ghat on July 12 [31] and also in the battle of Fatehgurh. Enfield rifle was issued to only British troops and according to Amin in 1857 there were only eight infantry and two cavalry regiments and thirteen batteries of artillery consisting of British troops. No native troops loyal to British and irregular cavalry was issued Enfield. In addition, even the British soldiers were not well acquainted with the new rifle. Havelock left about three thousand Enfield rifles in Allahabad as his soldiers were not accustomed to these rifles. In addition, in the early models of Enfield, bullets jammed so tightly the armourers were forced to bore them out. The high numbers on back sights were taken to indicate velocity instead of range. The result was an elevation that made fire ineffective. In many fiercely fought battles like the ones for capture of Delhi, and many strongholds of Lucknow (Kaiserbagh, Sikandarbagh and Shah Najaf) were frontal charges. Bayonets and close range fighting played a more significant role in these battles. Small fortifications in the cities, blocked streets and loophole walls and houses were taken from rebels by close fight.

At the onset of rebellion at one garrison showed some organization and discipline but it quickly dissipated. Mutiny, confusion, looting, murder and further confusion were a sequence which was tragically repeated in almost all areas with few exceptions. Even in one location there was no unified and organized effort by rebels to plan their actions. In Delhi, the troops, princes, court and commander-in-chief were all collecting funds from the people independently from one another. Only in areas, where a strong leader was able to exert some influence did an organized effort emerge but that was also transient. There were too many mutually exclusive sometimes hostile forces were at play in the rebel camp to allow for a large scale centralized effort against more organized British forces.

Social Aspect

The rebellion has to carefully evaluate as any generalization would lead to wrong conclusions. Overall, the rebellion did not have a clearly defined course and it differed markedly from region to region. Various overlapping factors were at play at same time thus making the task of well organized analysis very difficult. India of 1857 was not one country in modern sense but a collection of various areas inhabited by diverse groups. The rebellion was limited to certain areas and a large segment of the population remained loyal. A.H. Amin had discussed very eloquently this diversity and the reasons for rebellion or loyalty of various groups. As in any conflict, socio-economic factors play an important role but it is important to see them in proper perspective. Some authors have treated the subject appropriately while others have gone to the extreme to portray the whole event as an economic struggle launched by peasants on Marxist lines which is not true.

The rebellion was essentially by the previously dominant classes in the North-Western Provinces (North Western provinces consisted of eight divisions—Meerut, Delhi, Agra, Rohilkhand, Jhansi, Jabalpur, Allahabad and Banaras. Not to be confused with North West Frontier Province which was separated from Punjab in 1901), including both Hindus and Muslims. There is no doubt that a large number of people of India had grievances against the company government. In the early part of rebellion, many preferred to wait and watch rather than throw their lot with one side or another. They expected an aggressive and overwhelming response from the company army. The fact that 'the government had been caught off balance with its military resources stretched to breaking point', resulted in a slow or no response thus encouraging many to side with the rebels thinking that the company rule is coming to an end. This explains the second wave of mutinies in Lucknow, Cawnpur and Azamgurh, which occurred almost one month later than the Meerut uprising.

Several legislative measures of the company challenging centuries old traditions caused many apprehensions. Sutte (burning of widows on the pyres of their husbands) was abolished in 1829. James Ramsay, the 10th Earl of Dilhousie became Governor-General of India in 1847 and embarked on ambitious administrative reforms which will shake the foundations of centuries old customs of the ancient land. The thirty five years old workaholic Dalhousie reformed almost every aspect of the Company's rule in India. Several measures taken by the British in annexed areas raised the caste and religious feelings. These measures roused the suspicions of Hindus and Muslims alike. New legislative measures in 1856, allowing Hindu widows to re-marry raised Hindu suspicions. Enaction of laws allowing converts to inherit property caused doubts in both Hindu and Muslim minds. In early nineteenth century there was increasing missionary activity in India which was seen as an organized attempt of an alien group to let the natives stray away from their religions. British attempts to discourage early marriages and joint messing of convicts in jails and compulsory shaving were seen as intrusion into the traditional ways and an attempt of proselytizing. In 1855, Mr. Edmond issued a circular letter from Calcutta stating that in railway train no caste distinction will be made in the seating arrangements. Even in military, sepoys resented the efforts of some officers with missionary zeal.

These religious activities of Lt. Colonel G.S. Wheler of 34th BNI in Barrackpore and Major Mackenzie in Bolarum were directly responsible for the disaffection among the sepoys. The famous Mangal Pandey who fired at his officers on March 29 was from 34th BNI. In 1837, Persian was abolished as a language of the court thus making a large number of Muslims unemployed in Bengal. English magistrates replaced Muslims who were attached to courts as Qazis, Muftis. In Bengal, even under Muslim rulers, Hindus were employed as revenue officers. Hindus going ahead in education retained the jobs in newly anglicized revenue system. In early part of nineteenth century, the law barring appointment of any Indian to a post carrying an annual salary of 500 sterling pounds effectively curtailed any future prospects of a native under new government.

It should be remembered that east India Company was a commercial entity with the primary objective of increasing its revenue. Social and political fallout from their decisions and long-term negative effects were a low priority on the minds of the agents of the company. The annexation of Oudh in 1856 was the single act which thoroughly alienated almost all classes of that region, including rulers of native states, landed aristocracy, courtiers, sepoys and peasants. In north western provinces, British adopted the policy of not resuming the Jagirs after the death of the holder to its descendants. Instead, they gave the heirs fixed pension. From 1847 to 1856, the company in this way acquired Nagpur, Jhansi, Satara and Sambalpur.

In Bengal and northern India, landholders became fearful of their future under British. Similarly, the revenue free land holders in Bengal and North-Western Provinces came under scrutiny as the company wanted to increase its revenue base. In North Western Provinces, a large number of resumptions of revenue-free lands occurred between 1850 and 1856, causing a surge of anti-government sentiment.

In contrast, in Sindh, Napier made the landlords as the aristocracy of the land thus attaching their interest with the British, hence no unrest in Sindh during 1857. Talukdar (owners of large groups of villages) were powerful feudal barons and a recognized institution of nineteenth century Central India. They have been the intermediaries between the rulers and village proprietors for centuries. The land policies of British in North Western province removed the intermediary Talukdars. In Rohilkhand (This division consisted of Bareilly, Badaun, Bijnor, Muradabad and Shahjahanpur), many landed elites were Muslims. The new revenue policy disposed many of them. This powerful lot of landed aristocracy became hostile to British and British would pay with blood for this nearly fatal mistake.

The new set of village landowners though removed from the rapaciousness of the talukdars had their own grievances. The mix of specific complaints about revenue and taxes, cumbersome and lengthy new British judicial system and sharing of general anxieties of the public at large resulted in such an equation that the potential beneficiaries of new British policies ended up rallying around the old guard of landed elite. British courts gave legal protection to the money lenders (Mahajans) who were able to acquire landed interests which were confiscated. This was one of the reasons that everywhere, the rebels burned government revenue records, account books of money lenders and destroyed their property. In contrast to Delhi, where soldiers were in the forefront of resistance, in Lucknow it was the levies of talukdars rather than regular sepoys who gave the British tough fight. In 1852, an act was passed for scrutiny of rent-free tenures.

The tribunal called Inam Commission aggressively went after rent-free tenures. From 1852-57, in Southern Marhatta country alone about 35 thousand estates were called for and in 21 thousand cases sentences of confiscation were pronounced. In Bengal similar measures brought extra income of 5, 000, 000 sterling pounds per year while in Bombay it was 370, 000 sterling pounds per year. After the annexation of Oudh in 1856, a vigorous settlement policy was pursued which resulted in enormous social upheaval. In Cawnpur area, boats between Calcutta and Cawnpur transported most of goods. These boats were owned and operated by Hindus living in the vicinity of Sati Chowra Ghat. Their fortunes had been declining with the arrival of British as British-owned steamers, railways and Grand Trunk Road were taking away all their business. The middle of nineteenth century saw the end of the era of military adventurers, most of who were Muslims from northern India. After the Marhatta and Pindari wars, although good number of soldiers was enlisted in the Company army but still a large number became unemployed. In 1854, the number of these angry out of job soldiers was estimated to be 100, 000 in Rohilkhand and surrounding areas. When Wajid Ali Shah was deposed in February 1856, 200, 000 strong royal army was dispersed. Apart from soldiers, many others who depended on the army such as 12, 000 armourers became jobless. Later government ordered talukdars to dismiss their armed retainers thus resulting in swelling of number of unemployed who gradually drifted to large cities. These disgruntled ex-soldiers were now scattered all over Oudh.

Adding insult to injury, British dropped any pretense of respect to previous ruling class. In 1803, Shah Alam was a British pensioner with eleven and a half lakh rupees and ruling powers limited to the Red Fort area. This was a fact but for illiterate native, the King in Delhi still represented a mythical past of glory. Senior officers of East India Company omitted gradually all normal courtesies to a king. In 1844, nazar to King was abolished. In fact, in 1851, Bahadur Shah Zafar was receiving 833 rupees per month in lieu of his nazars. In 1820s, Heber wrote about the possibility of Muslims rising against the British but the reasons he argued will be political and not religious. One of the reasons which he mentioned was 'the conduct of Lord Hastings to the old emperor of Delhi'. The jewels of family of raja of Nagpur were sold in an auction in Calcutta. After annexation of Oudh, chief Commissioner used Umbrella Palace as stable for his horses. Similar measures at local levels in dealings with local elites caused resentment.

The role of Hindus and Muslims and their relationship with each other was also a complex phenomenon and varied from region to region. Hindus mostly led the civil risings in Oudh, Bihar, Gorakhpur and Central India. Many leaders of the uprising such as Nana Sahib, Tantia Topi and Rani of Jhansi were Hindus. After the rebellion was suppressed, land from Hindus was confiscated in large scale in Meerut, Jhansi, Etawa, Jabalpur which were the centres of Hindu dissatisfaction. In Patna and Bijnor, Muslims helped British to regain the control. In Rohilkhand, Fatehpur and Bulandshahar, the sites of Muslim discontent, confiscations were predominantly Muslim. Nawabs of Karnal, Muradabad, Dacca and Rampur and Nizam of Hyderabad remained loyal to British. Some confiscated land was awarded to the loyal subjects, both Hindu and Muslim and remainder auctioned off.

The relationships between Hindus and Muslims during the rebellion were complex and depended on local scene and the conduct of the local rebel leaders. In Rohilkhand, the rebels were almost exclusively Muslims (In Bijnor their leader was Nawab of Najibabad, Muhammad Khan and in Bareilly Khan Bahadur Khan). The rebels raised the green flag and used religious symbols. When the rebels robbed rich Hindu merchants and bankers, the cleavage lines between two communities widened. The worsening law and order situation in the area with bands of marauding gangs of Gujars, Maiwatis, Jats, Chauhans and Banjaras creating havoc culminated in a sanguine battle between Hindus and Muslims at Haldaur on September 18.44 In Malawa, Firuz Shah headed the rebellion.

The religious zeal attracted many Muslim tribes but alienated Hindus. In Cawnpur, the leadership by Nana Sahib roused the suspicion of influential Muslims. Initially, he arrested Nunne Nawab, an influential Muslim noble of Lucknow who had settled in Cawnpur. Later, under pressure, Nunne Nawab was not also released but made commander of a section of the force with artillery batteries. A crisis situation occurred when two Muslim butchers convicted of killing a cow died from bleeding when their hands were amputated. The sowars of 2nd Cavalry along with a large Muslim crowd confronted Nana and threatened to displace him. The showdown between Hindus and Muslims was averted by an apology from Nana and hectic efforts by his Muslim counsel, Azeemullah. Ironically, the last rebel stand against British was by a former government lawyer, a Hindu chief Ramnarayan at a place named Islamnagar.

The British rule in Punjab and Frontier had effectively ended the anarchy in Punjab and north western borders of India. The populace in general especially Muslims saw British rule as benign and peaceful. That is why, Muslims of these areas sided with British in 1857. Sikhs, Pathans and Muslims from Punjab rushed to India to fight side by side with British. The famous march of Guides from Mardan to Delhi is now a legend. William Hodson commanded a regiment of irregular horse of 300 Punjabi and Pathan troopers who were known as 'Plungers'. In areas, where the general population sentiment was not hostile to the British, the regiments which rebelled didn't succeed to damage the British. This was the case in Ferozpur, Ambala, Layyah, Mianwali and Peshawar. Ironically, the revolt of 1857 which is seen as a first organized attempt against colonial hegemony, 'established the Punjab as the bastion of colonialism and strengthened the basis of an authoritarian structure'. The results were far reaching as 'political institutions in the Punjab lagged behind their counterparts in the rest of the subcontinent'.

Native Players

Several authors had written a lot about the motives of different leaders of the rebellion. The opinion ranges from 'hatred' to 'some supreme national cause'. As related to other aspects of the rebellion any generalization in this particular area will lead to wrong conclusions. A. H. Amin had discussed this subject more rationally without much rhetoric but he seems to distribute the titles of 'patriot' and 'opportunist' a bit more casually. Each individual local leader of the rebellion had his or her particular reasons for joining the revolt. This was equally applicable to various groups who sided with the rebels. 'The sepoys fighting for fear of castes, the chiefs for their kingdoms, the landlords for their estates, the mass for fear of conversion and agrarian grievances, and the Muslims especially for restoring their old sway, yet all in their own way against the common enemy, the English'. Several tribal communities (Gujar, Jats, Palwars, Bhogtas, Maiwatis) joined simply due to the ample opportunity of plunder in a situation of a general breakdown of law and order.

India of 1857 was not a nation state in modern sense but a collection of various groups with autonomous local chiefs. Rebellion provided to many ambitious men an opportunity to act on their dreams of grandeur. Many rebel leaders invoked the name of old Mughal king of Delhi, but 'that was a pseudolegalistic ploy more than a real act of loyalty'. It is clear from several writings of British and natives that even the rebel sepoys in Delhi actually in contact with the king did not show any respect and talked to him rudely. They probably knew the real worth of the opium addicted statue of a dying era. Petty leaders set themselves up as rajas and even kings.

In Banawar, Qalandar Khan set himself as raja while Kadam Singh of Prachitgarh proclaimed himself king. Umrao Singh declared himself a raja after getting hold of one village of Manakpur while Fatua of Buddhakheri proclaimed himself king of the Gujars. Rao Bhopal Singh at the head of his Chauhan followers declared a Rajput government but poor fellow was surprised at his place and promptly executed. Others like rajas of Kutra and Mainpuri, Apa Sahib, Shahamal and his grandson Lujjram (Jat) of Baraut, Narpat Singh (Rajput) of Akulpur enjoyed the power and fame for few months.

We will probably never know the real motive of a particular local chief to join the rebels or British. Probably several factors may be at play in each case when the critical hour of decision came to choose one's bet. Most of local chiefs which sided with rebels were in the vicinity of Delhi. Abdurrahman of Jhajjar, Hassan Ali Khan of Dojana, Nahar Singh of Ballabgarh, Tularam of Rewari, Walidad Khan of Malagarh and Ahmad Ali Khan of Farrukh Nagar. The Rajput chiefs of Jaipur, Bikanir and Alwar were not much interested in re-surrecting the decaying Mughal rule. The political rivals of local chiefs who sided with British decided to take a chance and sided with rebels. The Maharajah of Jodhpur, Takht Singh sided with British offering his troops. His rival Thakur Kushai Singh worked on Jodhpur Legion which deserted to the mutineers. Mohammad Hassan took control of Gorakhpur rallying disgruntled landed elites although he had no mutinous troops. He was the former governor of Gorakhpur and had lost his position after the annexation of Oudh. Similarly, the Chief of Nargund, Baba Sahib in Southern Marhatta country, who was denied the right of adoption declared war in May 1858 when British were re-asserting themselves after initial setbacks. It was mainly civil uprising as no mutinous troops were involved in the conflict.

In Rohilkhand, Mahmud Khan of Najibabad waited till all areas including Bareilly, Muradabad, Mandawar had rebelled and almost all British officers were killed or had fled to safety. Seeing the changed winds, many locals gathered around Mahmud Khan as he seemed to be poised to take control of the area. When Mahmud arrived in Bijnor on June 7, he had about 200-250 Pathan musketeers with him.

There is no detailed account of the exploits of several local leaders of the rebellion like Mehdi Hassan of Sultanpur, Fazal Azim of Rae Bareli, Banda Hussain a Lt. of Mehdi Hassan, Rao Sahib, Moulvi Sarfaraz Ali of Gorakhpur, Moulvi Sikander Shah of Faizabad, Ghaus Mohammad Khan of Sikandra Rao and Kunwar Singh.

Tantia Topi though with no military experience, learned the art of war on the field. Tantia was six years older than Nana Sahib and his playmate. He arranged for the defence of Bithur, the toughest challenge to Havelock's force. He repelled Windham's assault on Cawnpur. He later made unsuccessful attempt to relieve the siege of Jhansi. Even after the setbacks, he was one of the few who appreciated the opponent's weakness. This resulted in a fast moving guerrilla warfare in Nagpur and Gwalior in the summer of 1858. Unfortunately, this 'display of tactical brilliance was too late to influence the outcome of a war which had already been decided by British victories at Delhi and Oudh'. He was betrayed by Raja of Nawar (Raja rebelled against British but when the pendulum swung in their favour, he betrayed Tantia to re-habilitate himself) and hanged.

Nana Sahib was born as Govind Dhondu Pant and was the adopted son of Peshwa Baji Rao. When Baji Rao died in 1851, the company according to an earlier ruling of not recognizing the adopted sons of a deceased ruler stopped Baji Rao's pension. Nana Sahib was deprived of not only his pension but also hollow titles, his seal and yearly allocation of even blank cartridges for his guards. Next few years Nana kept sending petitions to the Company for resumption of his pension while entertaining British officers at his palace in Bithur without any success. The ideas of Azimullah Khan to attempt to recover his throne and predictions of his guru, Dassa Bawa that one day he will be victorious and his own dreams of grandeur may have effected him to take a bold course of siding with the rebels.

Azimullah Khan was another figure which appeared on the scene of rebellion and had a very interesting background. During the famine of 1837, as a starving boy along with his mother, he was given shelter at the mission at Cawnpur. He attended the free school and became fluent in English and French. After working with several Englishmen, he was hired as translator by Brigadier John Scott. After the death of Baji Rao, he was in the court of Nana Sahib. When Nana chose Azimullah to go to England to plead his case, a search started for an experience guide to accompany him. An educated Rohilkhand noble Muhammad Ali Khan had visited England in the employ of King of Nepal. Muhammd Ali had no love for the British. He was a bright young man and passed the Calcutta Civil Service examinations with flying colours.

Being a native, he was hired as a foreman where his arrogant superior insulted and humiliated him. He resigned the service in 1851 and ended up accompanying King of Nepal on a three month tour of England. In England, the intelligent Azimullah dressed in western outfit impressed many luminaries of the time. He met John Stuart Mill and the wife of Prime Minister's cousin who was gentleman Usher to the Queen, Lucie Gordon. He met Dickens, Carlyle, Macaulay, Tennyson and Thackery and had seen the Queen. He was probably the only Indian of his time who with the intelligence and the opportunity to visit the land of his masters was able to evaluate British.

The awe of the British which was maintained in India was to be shaken. The splendid city of London was actually smothered with industrial smoke. He was unable to convince the authorities to resume his master's pension but on his journey back, he stopped in Constantinople and visited the battlefield of Crimea and brought with him a French printing press. Although his mission failed but he had come back with a more dangerous idea. He presented a more ambitious agenda for Nana, telling him 'why worry about his measly stipend when he might annihilate the English and recover his throne?'

The former dancing girl and later the Queen Hazrat Mahal's behaviour was more praiseworthy than her debauch husband, Wajid Ali Shah. Wajid when told about his exile was 'weeping, pleading, baring his head to the appalled and embarrassed Colonel Outram. On the contrary, in November when a shell hit the palace gate, the garrison panicked and soldiers fled away. The indomitable Hazrat Mahal remained staunch and when told chiefs to cut her head before running away, they stayed feeling the shame and humiliation.

On another occasion, she sent a pair of women's trousers to a faint-hearted chief with a note stating that better he should put them on and to retire to his proper place — a harem. She spent 50, 000 sterling pounds of her own money to build a wall around the city. She had the rare leadership qualities to gain the confidence of both Hindus and Muslims. She was able to prevent the division between two communities due to the activities of religious zealots like Moulvi Massih-us-Zaman and Babar Ali. In this effort, she was helped by Moulvi Ahmadullah Shah, who not only worked for cooperation between Hindus and Muslims but between Shias and Sunnis of Lucknow. She was able to rally the soldiers, landed nobility and city population to her cause. In middle of 1859, when the rebel cause seemed to be doomed, Hazarat Mahal and her two staunch Hindu allies, Beni Mado and Hanumant Singh refused to surrender to British.

Lakshmibai, the Rani of Jhansi's role is somewhat controversial. Although she along with several local chiefs had grievances against British, it has not been proven that she had any role in the mutiny of 12th BNI and 13th Irregular cavalry stationed at Jhansi on June 5th. She had to pay ransom to the rebels before they left Jhansi. In fact on June 12 and 14, she wrote letters to Erskine, the commissioner of Sagar division assuring him that she would hold Jhansi on behalf of the British. Erskine in a formal letter authorized her to collect the revenue.

She led her troops against the Dewan of Orchha, an old rival. This suggests that in the early part of the rebellion when she was quite vulnerable to both British and rival chieftain's attack, she favoured siding with British but later the ambiguous British diplomacy and declining of her protestations of loyalty that she decided to fight the British. She personally commanded the defence of Jhansi working with the defenders who consisted of mutineers, levies and mercenaries. She not only showed her superior administrative and military skills but also personal bravery in combat. She only trusted the five hundred Kabuli Pathans of her army, who escorted her after her defeat at Jhansi. She earned the respect and praise of even her enemies when she died on the battlefield at Gwalior.

In Bareilly, the garrison rebelled on May 31, 1857. After the routine of initial confusion, disorder, looting and killing, Khan Bahadar Khan was proclaimed leader. He was the grandson of a revered Rohilla chief. Interestingly, the army in and around Bareilly was the largest, about 57 regiments with gunners and sappers. Despite that there does not seem to be a close cooperation among military and civil leadership of the rebellion to take advantage of this huge difference in balance of power. There were tensions between the civil leader Khan Bahadar and military leader Bakht Khan. Bakht Khan was smart and had taken control of the Bareilly treasury. He calculated his odds and with the treasury and the strength of a brigade under his command, he had a better chance at Delhi. Once in Delhi, with both the money and sepoys, the confidant Bakht

Khan approached Bahadur Shah Zafar and asked the old king to appoint him commander-in-chief which the king obliged. Unfortunately, in Delhi, he found his nemesis. The commander of Nimach rebels, Muhammad Ghaus Khan became his bitter rival thus preventing a unified stand of the rebels.

Conclusion

1857 was the watershed in the history of subcontinent. It was such a confusing catalogue of events that to decipher them individually would be an impossible task. On one hand, the rebels were destroying everything attached to the British rule like bungalows, telegraph, official records while on the other the rebel troops fought in their red uniforms under their regimental colours, kept their muster roll update and wore the medals awarded by British.

In one instance at Cawnpur, Havelock encountered a rebel unit whose band was playing Auld Lang Syne. The immediate effect after the rebellion was the change of colonial thought process. Prior to 1857, 'The British viewed India as a social laboratory for transformation in the former's image—a social revolution which would change backward India into a modern society along the lines of an intrinsically western model'.

The blend of 'nationalism and evangelism' of British had convinced them that it was God's will which they were fulfilling. They sincerely believed that with the marvels of modernism, railways and telegraph, they will 'bring or drag reluctant India into the modern world'. The great revolt was a kind of rude awakening for the British. British officials saw the revolt as a consequence of upsetting of the social status quo of India by British policies. In post-1857 period, 'enlightment was no longer a priority and maintenance of law and order became the essence of future British policy in India'. In British mind, the native Indian population was divided into two groups. The groups which ignited the revolt (Brahmins and

Muslims of Oudh) were seen as cunning and untrustworthy and were awarded the punishment they deserved.

The groups (Sikhs, Muslims of Punjab and Frontier, Princely states) which sided with British were considered loyal and appropriately rewarded. It is clear now that if the loyal natives had not helped John Lawrence in Punjab, Edwards and Davidson in Hyderabad, Gubbins in Benaras, Robert Ellis in Nagpur and Osborne in Rewa, the Indian history would be different. The lessons of rebellion of 1857 are not interesting for historians only but leaders of post-colonial states have to ponder over the blunders made hundred and fifty years ago. The reason for this advice is the fact that both civil and military leadership especially in Pakistan has more of a colonial mind set rather than the thought process of an independent nation.

Igniting the Powder Keg

The fears of the sepoys were easily played upon by those who hoped to persuade them to turn their guns against the British. There were reports of nocturnal meetings in the barracks. Mysterious fires broke out, burning arrows were shot into the thatched roofs of officers' bungalows, and the telegraph station at the great military post of Barrackpore near Calcutta was burned down. Most mysterious of all, flat cakes of flour and water known as chapatis were passed from village to village. A messenger would arrive bearing them, saying that they had been brought to his own village and must be passed on. In time, the news of this strange ritual reached the British officials. What could it mean? Some argued that it was a method of carrying away disease, though there was no epidemic in 1857. When Indians were questioned, some said the distribution of chapatis meant that something terrible would happen, but they did not know what it might be. Others replied that they believed the chapatis were distributed by order of the British, and had not thought to inquire further. Whatever it meant, no one dared to disobey the summons to pass the flat cakes on to the next village, and with the chapatis there spread throughout the land the feeling of expectancy, of tension, of uneasiness.

All of these incidents were reported, and the reports were passed up through various levels of authority until they ultimately arrived on the table of the Governor General. In the highly centralized system of British administration, everything had to be committed to paper and no action could be taken until it had been approved by a higher authority. A torrential flood of paper flowed endlessly towards the Governor-General's office, silting up the channels of communication, stifling all initiative.

Very few, even among the most senior military officers, were prepared to bypass the system. One who did was General John Hearsey, commanding at Barrackpore. As early as the end of January, 1857 he had directly warned the Governor General that there were persons at work deliberately creating trouble among the sepoys, and that something must be done. But even then, the system took control and delayed decision. Early in February, Hearsey decided to take action himself. He ordered a parade of the sepoys at Barrackpore at which he himself would try to reassure them that the British had no designs on their religion.

Hearsey had the advantage of long service in India; in fact he had been born there. He was now 66 years of age, and his military life had been spent with the sepoys of the Company's army. He was one of the few senior officers who respected the sepoys and received, in return, their respect and affection. Though old by Indian standards, he was still strong and active, a good horseman with a commanding presence. If anyone could persuade the sepoys of the good intentions of the government it was Hearsey. He spoke to the assembled men on February 9 in their own language. His arguments were simple and fluent, and the sepoys believed him.

Unfortunately, Hearsey could not speak at every military station. Too often a commander, instead of using persuasion - and, if that failed, taking decisive action - panicked.

Such was the case with a Colonel Mitchell, commanding the military station at Berhampur, some 90 miles to the north of Barrackpore. There were no European troops on the station, only the 19th Native Infantry, a squadron of native cavalry, and a battery of guns manned by sepoys. At a parade on February 27, the infantrymen refused to accept an issue of cartridges which they believed were of the new contaminiated kind, though in fact they were not. Instead of attempting to reassure his men, Colonel Mitchell, hurrying to the parade ground, threatened to take the regiment to Burma or to China. Overseas travel was another way that Sepoys believed that they would lose Caste. The sepoys took their commander's angry threats as proof that all the rumours they had heard were true, and their discipline broke. At this point Mitchell became conciliatory, for he feared that the gunners and cavalry might be equally mutinous. The sepoys returned to their duties, retaining their arms. Colonel Mitchell reported the events to Calcutta, and the system finally ground out a decision on March 23 that the 19th Native Infantry should be marched down to Barrackpore, to be disbanded under the eyes of a British regiment, Her Majesty's 87th, which was hastily being brought back from Burma.

That British troops had to be brought from such a distance merely emphasized how few there were in northern India. Most of the European troops assigned to Bengal had been moved west to secure the Punjab when it had been conquered and annexed eight years earlier. At Calcutta there was one British infantry battalion, and another was stationed 400 miles away at Dinapur. One regiment was stationed at Agra, and one at Lucknow. Altogether, in Bengal - an area as large as France and Germany combined - the British in the Company troops and the Queen's forces (lent to the Company by the

Crown) amounted to only four infantry battalions and a few individual batteries of artillery. The Queen's forces had already been considerably reduced because of the demands of the Crimean War then raging between Britain and its allies against Russia. In India as a whole, there were about 4,000 Europeans in the Company and royal armies, as compared with a total strength of about 300,000 Indian soldiers.

When the news of the impending disbandment of Mitchell's command reached the sepoys at Barrackpore, their faith in the assurances of General Hearsey began to evaporate. A rumour reached the British that on March 10, when the Governor-General and the most important British officers would be attending a fete to be given by the Maharaja of Gwalior, there was to be a general uprising by the sepoys. Because of an unseasonable downpour of rain, the entertainment was cancelled. The day passed without incident, but the rumours of rebellion persisted. The Governor-General was anxious. So was General Hearsey, who decided to address the sepoys under his command once again. Among the rumours at Barrackpore was one that British troops of the 87th, due in shortly from Burma, were to make a sudden attack on the sepoys. On March 17, Hearsey once again reassured his troops: they need not fear for their caste or their religion, he said, for the Europeans were coming only to disband the mutinous 19th Native Infantry.

But the imminent punishment of the 19th - who by refusing the cartridge had steadfastly remained loyal to their faith - had already made a deep impression on Hearsey's sepoys. Nine days later, as he sat in his bungalow, Hearsey received news of a tumult on the parade ground. After sending orders to the British troops to stand by, the General rode to the scene, accompanied by his son John. A shocking sight met his eyes. A young sepoy named Mangal Pande had just cut down two European officers and was now calling on his comrades to rebel and die bravely for their religion. No one seemed to be taking action. In one corner stood a group of

British officers, including the commander of the sepoys' regiment, all apparently struck with paralysis. One of these men called out to Hearsey: *"Have a care! His musket is loaded." "Damn his musket"* replied Hearsey, and added to his son: *"If I fall, John, rush in and put him to death somehow!"*

As the General rode towards him, the sepoy raised his musket - then turned it on himself and pulled the trigger. But he only succeeded in wounding himself, and after being taken prisoner was court-martialled, condemned and hanged. His name lived on, for soon the cry of "Remember Mangal Pandey I" was to become the Indians signal for revolt, and for the British "pandy" became a general term of abuse for all Mutineers.

The 19th were disarmed and disbanded without incident at the end of March, and the Commander-in-Chief, General George Anson, saw no reason to alter the usual hot-weather routine of the army. Despite continuing reports of barracks mysteriously going up in flames and of secret meetings among the sepoys, European troops were marched to cooler stations in the foothills of the Himalayas. Officers went on leave. General Anson - who had seen no fighting since the war against Napoleon more than 40 years earlier retired with his staff to the hill-station of Simla, nearly 1,000 miles away from the Governor-General and the civil government in Calcutta.

The officers and their families in the cool of their hill retreats had no means of knowing it, but down on the plains, in the great military cantonment of Meerut, 40 miles outside Delhi, greater troubles were brewing. There, 85 sepoys had refused to accept the new cartridge. They had been court-martialled and found guilty of disobedience and sentenced to varying terms of imprisonment with hard labour. On Saturday, May 9, the whole garrison was paraded to witness the sentences being put into effect.

For one young lieutenant, Hugh Gough, who afterwards wrote a vivid account of the Mutiny outbreak, the events of that day seemed heavy with foreboding. Even the weather underlined the menace, for it was dark, with low clouds, and a hot dry wind blowing across the parade ground where some 4,000 men were drawn up to form three sides of a hollow square. The sombre light seemed to heighten the silver-grey of Gough's own 3rd Light Cavalry, the shining brass helmets and leather breeches of the Bengal Artillery officers, the black horsehair plumes of the Dragoon Guards, the olive-green of the 60th Native Rifles, and the scarlet coats and white collars of the Native Infantry.

On the fourth, open side of the square stood the 85 sepoys. They were clad in their uniforms, but their feet were bare and they carried no weapons. Their comrades, rigid at attention, carried arms, but everyone knew that their ammunition pouches were empty - by order. The British troops had their rifles, the new Enfields loaded with the cartridges that had caused all the trouble, and aimed at the Native Infantry. Gaps in their ranks showed the open mouths of guns, at each breech a gunner at the ready.

A British officer stepped forward and a ripple ran through the ranks. Slowly he read from a paper, an Indian officer translating his words into careful Hindustani. When they had finished there was silence for a moment, then a party of British soldiers moved down the file ripping the buttons from the uniforms of the 85 sepoys and the coats from their backs. Armourers with tools and shackles came forward and slowly began to fit fetters on the condemned men, many of whom had served the British government with perfect loyalty through long years and bloody battles. As the fetters were placed upon them, they lifted up their hands, beseeching the General to have mercy on them, but seeing no hope there they turned to their comrades and reproached them for standing aside and allowing them to be disgraced. Many of them were in tears, but they could do nothing in the face of the loaded field-guns and rifles, and the glittering sabres of the Dragoons. For a moment, it seemed to Lieutenant Gough as if the sepoys were about to attack the British with their bare hands; but the prisoners were marched off and the tension eased.

That evening Gough went down to the temporary jail and was deeply moved by the grief of the men who begged him to save them. Later, in the dark of the veranda, he wondered what would happen next. His thoughts were interrupted by a rustle in the darkness. It was a native officer of his own troop who had come, he said, to discuss the troops' accounts. Gough found this odd, especially as the man seemed frightened and kept carefully to the shadows. Then the real purpose of the visit was revealed. Tomorrow, Sunday, the sepoys would mutiny - all of them, even the cavalry, the sahib's own men. They would break open the jail and release their comrades. Death was planned for the white soldiers and their families.

After the man had left, Gough went to the mess and informed his colonel, George Carmichael-Smyth. His story was greeted with laughter. When he had been in India a little longer, he would learn not to take such stories seriously. But Gough was convinced that the native officer had come to warn him of a real danger. He went to the Brigadier commanding the station, Archdale Wilson, and was treated with good-natured contempt. If no one else was worried, why should Lieutenant Gough concern himself?

The next day was May 10, 1857. About 5 p.m. a rumour spread in Meerut bazaar that British troops were coming to seize the sepoys' arms. Sepoys in the bazaar hurried back to their barracks as an angry mob of villagers surged out to attack the Europeans' bungalows. On the parade ground, sepoys intent on releasing their imprisoned comrades slipped away from white officers desperately trying to control them. 'When Gough went out on his veranda an hour later the horizon was a sea of flame. Galloping down to the cavalry lines, he found *"a thousand sepoys dancing and leaping frantically about, calling and yelling to each other and blazing away with their muskets in all directions."*

By nightfall, Meerut was a city of horror. British officers had been cut down by their own men. Two officers' wives were murdered in incidents which acquired particular notoriety. One of them, a Mrs. Chambers, was pregnant; her unborn child was ripped from her womb by a local butcher. The other, a Mrs. Dawson, was recovering from smallpox; to avoid contagion, the mob threw burning torches at her until her clothes caught fire and burnt her to death.

The suddenness of the attack caught the senior officers off balance. Most were old, and had not had to fight since their youth. Though there were as many British troops in Meerut as there were Indians, and though the British had artillery, nothing was done to organize a response. Some of the younger officers, like Gough, tried to give their seniors a sense of urgency. But the mutineers were able to break open the jail, release the 85 prisoners and set off on the road to Delhi, 40 miles away to the south-west, unmolested by the British.

No one pursued them, and next morning the first of them reached the old imperial capital. Some went to the palace, the great red sandstone fort from which the Mughal emperors had ruled all India before the coming of the British. Bahadur Shah, the last of the Mughal line, now called - by courtesy of the British, who paid him a pension - "King of Delhi," did not welcome the sepoys, though they hailed him, as his ancestors had been hailed, "Emperor of Hindustani." But inside the palace there were also men who had waited long for an opportunity to do something against the British who had usurped the Mughal power. They welcomed the sepoys as liberators, and all the romantic appeal of a once great native dynasty rising again was grafted on to the confused aims of the mutineers.

There was little or nothing that the few British officers

and civilians in Delhi could do against the three native regiments stationed there, the mutineers from Meerut and the retainers of the King. The arsenal, one of the largest in India, was inside the city walls and guarded only by native troops. The main magazine was some three miles outside the city, having been moved there a few years earlier for added security. That, too, was guarded by native infantry. By nightfall of May 11, the Europeans in Delhi were in a bad way. Some escaped, some were prisoners in the palace, but many had been killed either by their own men or when the arsenal was blown up to prevent it from falling into the hands of the mutineers. The magazine however remained intact and was handed over to the mutineers; its 3,000 barrels of powder were saved to sustain the mutineers for three months against the forthcoming counter-attacks of the British.

Yet all was not well for the rebels inside the city. They set up an alternative government, a *"Court of Mutineers,"* but it was torn by rivalries between the various factions. Hindus, Muslims, sepoys, civilians and Mughal princes. All treated the Emperor, who was little more than a reluctant symbol of revolt, with open contempt. He even had to threaten suicide to save his closest confidant from death. Many princes preferred to play for safety by casting their lot with the British, now belatedly gathering their forces to strike back at the rebels. It became increasingly clear that the disunited force of mutineers would have very little chance of resisting a strong counter-attack.

A Year of Bloodshed

On the evening of May 12, General Anson was host to a Simla dinner party of 25. The wine and the talk were good, and when he was handed a telegram, he set it aside under hjs plate. When the ladies had left the table, he opened the flimsy blue form. It was from Delhi, *"We must leave office,"* he read. *"All the bungalows are on fire, burning down by the sepoys of Meerut. They came in this morning. Mr. C. Todd is dead, we think. He went out this morning and has not yet returned. We learn that nine Europeans were killed. We are off. Goodbye."* Already, two days had been lost. The telegraph was new to India and the line from Delhi went no further than Ambala, a distance of 66 miles from Simla.

The news, though it did not shock Anson into moving down into the plains himself, at least drove him into sending others. But it took time. Troops had to be rounded up from the various hill resorts. Meanwhile, the general wrote to Governor-General Canning that he awaited more information before he would proceed to Ambala. When the news came, the worst fears were confirmed.

On May 15, Anson and a force of some 6,000 men left for Ambala to organize the recapture of Delhi.

The task was formidable. Anson had the troops, but little ammunition and no transport. In an excess of economy, the army had lost its transport department some time pefore and had now to depend on civilian contractors. As no campaigns were ever mounted in the hot weather, much of the transport had been dispersed. As for ammunition, most of it had been stored in the great magazine at Delhi, which was thought to be secure.

While at Ambala, Anson was bombarded with telegrams-from the Governor-General, who ordered him to *"make as short work as possible of the rebels who have cooped themselves up in Delhi"* and from John Lawrence in the Punjab. Lawrence had himself moved ruthlessly against the rebels there. Now he wanted further action. Delhi would open its gates at the approach of British troops, he assured Anson. *"Pray only reflect on the whole history of India. Where have we failed when we acted vigorously? Where have we succeeded when guided by timid counsels?"*

Such advice was not a great deal of use to Anson, but he did move, with only 20 rounds of ammunition a man, and none for his artillery, without medical supplies and with no bullocks to pull the guns. The whole of the little force reached

Rarnal, some eight miles from Delhi, by May 30.

Three days earlier, Anson had died of cholera after handing over command to Sir Henry Barnard, who had at least seen action in the Crimea. Barnard decided to march without delay, supported by a reinforcement from Meerut under Archdale Wilson. Together, they met a force of mutineers some six miles from Delhi at Badli-ki-serai. After a sharp engagement on June 8, the British put the mutineers to flight. Elated with this initial success, Barnard and his troops moved on to Delhi.

The British occupied the old military cantonments outside the city, on what was known as the Ridge. As a gesture of defiance, they burnt the barracks - and left themselves without shelter from the grinding sun which was to beat down upon them for over three months in the hottest season of the Indian year. It was soon obvious that the British were not strong enough to take Delhi. The force on the Ridge numbered about 5,000 men, while the mutineers in the city had over 30,000, a figure increasing every day as more and more reinforcements came in brigades of cavalry and infantry, their regimental colours bearing the names of British victories flying bravely, their bands blaring British marching tunes. The British lacked not only men and guns but also dynamic leadership; heatstroke and cholera took a heavy toll. General Barnard himself succumbed early in July, and his successor was soon too ill to exercise command. The next senior officer was Archdale Wilson, hardly an encouraging replacement for he it was who had hesitated so fatally at Meerut.

The British had to have reinforcements and heavy artillery with which to breach the walls of Delhi, and the reinforcements could only come from the Punjab. Fortunately, there was John Lawrence who, while ensuring the safety of the Punjab, set in motion preparations for reinforcing the British outside Delhi with a massive siege-train: great guns drawn by 16 elephants and accompanied by over 500 waggons bursting with ammunition sufficient, it was confidently stated, *"to grind Delhi to powder."*

In the meantime, reinforcements had been steadily arriving and, with them, some younger officers anxious for action. Among them was John Nicholson. His reputation was already high, and one officer claimed that he was "an army in himself," but he was also quite sombre and humourless, and his presence cast *"a damper on the gaiety of some who sat around him"* in the Mess.

Nicholson was anxious to get on with the assault. But though Nicholson and others successfully mounted a number of small engagements, there was no possibility of assaulting the city, protected as it was by seven miles of walls, until the siege-train arrived. It did so on September 4, and three days later the first breaching battery was laid against the city walls. By the evening of the 14th, the British had broken into the city but the victory required bitter fighting and many casualties.

That night the guns were quiet, but the British soldiers found and broke open the cellars of merchants dealing in European liquors. One eyewitness wrote: *"A black or a green bottle filled with beer or wine or brandy was more precious than a tiara of diamonds."* Most of the British force spent two days in an orgy of violence, drunkeness and confusion, *"utterly demoralized" wrote Captain William Hodson, "by hard work and hard drink .... For the first time in my life, I have had to see English soldiers refuse repeatedly to follow their officers."*

When Archdale Wilson finally ordered the remaining liquor stores to be destroyed, there was still much to do in clearing the city of the remaining rebels, but by September 20, the city was in the hands of the British. The inhabitants were driven out into the countryside while the city was given over to plunder.

Meanwhile, elsewhere, the Mutiny had spread. Soon after the fall of Delhi to the mutineers, the British communities in two other cities, Lucknow and Cawnpore, in the former

Kingdom of Oudh, were threatened with extinction.

Here, 250 miles south-east of Delhi, the British were faced not only with a military rebellion but with what seemed like a mass revolt. The former King of Oudh was in comfortable exile in Calcutta, but his subjects remained behind in chaos and poverty. The state forces had been disbanded and armed soldiers had turned to banditry. The thousands of servants and tradesmen who had been employed by the King were left without a livelihood. New taxes pressed heavily on the people. A new tax on the use of opium drove thousands of addicts to suicide.

The Mutiny Spreads

During April, the British in Lucknow had made preparations for the coming crisis. In charge was Sir Henry Lawrence, brother of John. Under his guidance, the Residency was fortified. It stood to the north of the city on a raised plateau backing on to the River Gumti, and contained a number of buildings, offices and bungalows. All round this area were mosques and houses which overlooked the defences, giving fine vantage points for would-be attackers. Despite requests by his officers, Lawrence refused to demolish the Indian buildings. From any sound military viewpoint, then, the Residency was almost indefensible.

When the news of the outbreak at Meerut reached Lucknow, the situation immediately became dangerous. Buildings were set on fire, and armed Indians began to gather in the city and to attack European positions. By early June, the thin web of British rule had been broken. *"Every outpost, I fear, has fallen,"* wrote Lawrence on June 12, *"and we daily expect to be besieged by the confederated mutineers and their allies."*

Forty-two miles away at Cawnpore, another garrison was already fighting for its life. Cawnpore was the headquarters of the command that covered Oudh. In charge was Major-General Sir Hugh Wheeler. A man in his early seventies, he had served in India for 54 years - and none of them had prepared him for what he was now to face. Cawnpore was a large station, with many European and Eurasian families. To protect them Wheeler had only 60 European artillerymen, on whom he could rely absolutely. The rest of his troops were Indian.

There were two possible strong points, One was the magazine, which contained large stocks of weapons and ammunition. It stood only a little way from the river, which could have been used for a getaway in an emergency. The other consisted of two barrack buildings in the open, well away from the river, near the main road from Allahabad. The barracks, which had no defences, were chosen and surrounded by an inadequate entrenchment, though to a competent soldier the disadvantages of the position should have been obvious.

Near Cawnpore, in the town of Bithur, lived a man known as the Nana Sahib. The Nana was the adopted son of a prince who, after defeat by the British, had been settled in luxurious exile at Bithur, For 33 years the British paid the Ptince a lavish pension; but when he died in 1851 they refused to continue paying it to his adopted son. To Nana's appeals the government turned a deaf ear. The Nana, living in indolence and luxury in his palace - even financing his own body of troops - bided his time. Noone seemed to suspect that he might harbour a deep grudge against the British. He remained on the friendliest terms with the British and, in particular, with General Wheeler and his Indian wife. It is probable that the General asked his advice and received an assurance that, should the sepoys mutiny, they would make for Delhi and leave the British in Cawnpore alone. Certainly, Wheeler trusted the Nana implicitly; after deciding on the barracks as his own defensive position, the General invited him to take over the magazine and the Treasury with his household troops!

The Nana occupied these two points and waited. On the night of June 4 nearly all of the sepoys mutinied, burning their barracks before looting the Treasury. Some of those who did not do so joined Wheeler inside the entrenchment. The mutineers - as the Nana had foretold left for Delhi. Wheeler felt that all he had to do was wait for reinforcements, which he expected at any moment. He was soon disillusioned. The sepoys had halted only a few miles up the road.

On June 6, Wheeler received a letter from the Nana Sahib saying that he intended to attack the entrenchment. Within a few hours the area was surrounded by the rebels, and the guns from the magazine that Wheeler had handed over to his friend were dropping roundshot on the barracks. Behind a feeble rampart four feet high and made of loose earth were 240 men and 375 women and children. The sun was at its hottest, gunbarrels burned the hand that held them, and there was little or no protection though about 60 years later a huge underground room was discovered below the barracks that would have given cool and bullet-proof protection. Unaware of its existence, the garrison was protected from the mutineers' heavy artillery fire only by shallow trenches.

The death-toll among the defenders grew steadily. On June 23, the anniversary of the Battle of Plassey, a great assault was beaten off. But food and water were scarce, and the route to the well was open to heavy fire from the mutineers. By June 25 the ammunition was almost gone and starvation confronted the garrison in the face. There was no sign of relief, but on the same day the Nana offered terms of surrender. Wheeler himself was opposed to surrender, but others thought that some attempt should be made to save the women and children.

A written treaty was drafted and accepted, by which the British were to surrender their guns and treasure and theIil march out of the entrenchment with their hand-arms and 60 rounds of ammunition for each man. The Nana was to provide boats to transport the women, the children and the sick.

On June 27 what remained of the garrison marched out towards the landingstage. The sick and the women were carried out in palanquins, and the children who could not walk were carried'by some of the sepoys who had been trying to kill them a few days before. By 9 a.m. all were embarked in large clumsy vessels with thatched roofs which looked, from a distance, *"rather like floating haystacks."* Suddenly, and without warning, a shot was heard. Fearful of treachery, and with nerves tattered by three weeks of siege, the British immediately opened fire. The Nana's men replied with grapeshot and ball, and the little fleet was soon ablaze. One boat succeeded in getting away, and four of its occupants finally reached safety.

Of those who survived this last battle, the men - 60 in number - were killed by the Nana's troops; the women and children were first imprisoned in a large house and later moved to a smaller one built by an English officer for his native mistress (hence its name, Bibighur, meaning "House of Ladies"). On July 15th, news reached Cawnpore that the British were approaching the city. Nana Sahib ordered all the remaining prisoners to be killed. His motives for doing this remain obscure. Perhaps it was out of blind rage, perhaps to rid himself of those who might give evidence against him, perhaps in the extraordinary belief that the approaching forces would then have no remaining motive to press home their assault in order to rescue their imprisoned countrymen.

Towards evening, five British men fugitives from elsewhere captured over the past few days - were taken out and shot. Then a party of sepoys was detailed off to execute the 210 women and children. Apparently unable to bring themselves to commit such cold-blooded murder, they-fired high. Butchers were then summoned from the bazaar and together with two or three of the Nana's troops went in to finish the job with knives. It was not efficiently done. A few were still alive in the morning, among them some children, saved perhaps, by the crush of bodies in the darkness. In the morning, the victims were dragged out and thrown down a near-by well. Some sepoys said that the children still alive were killed first, others that they were tossed alive into the well.

It was this atrocity above all which inflamed British feelings when the relief forces under General Henry Havelock arrived to begin the assault on Cawnpore two days later.

The recapture of Cawnpore was the first stage on the way to relieving the Residency at Lucknow. The 2,000 troops, racked by dysentery, cholera and heatstroke, took ten days to advance the 100 miles from Allahabad to Cawnpore. When they entered the town, on the 17th, they still hoped to bring release to the women and children imprisoned there. Instead they found a slaughter-house. *"I am not exaggerating,"* wrote one officer, *"when I tell you that the soles of my boots were more than covered with the blood of these poor wretched creatures."* Blood-stained clothing was scattered about, as well as leaves ripped out of the Bible and out of another appropriately titled book, *Preparation for Death.*

The British left the room untouched, and filled in the well only partially; so that they could stand as terrible reminders to new troops from England that their duty must be sustained by a desire for revenge. One soldier, his head full of tales of atrocities, reported: *"I seed two Moors [Indians] talking in a cart. Presently I heard one of 'em say 'Cawnpore.' I knowed what that meant; so I fetched Tom Walker, and he heard 'em say 'Cawnpore,' and he knowed what that meant. So we polished 'em both off."*

Revenge was not confined to ignorant soldiers. At Cawnpore, Brigadier-General James Neill issued an order on July 25 that every captured rebel, whether proved guilty or not, *"will be taken down to the house and will be forced to clean up a small portion of the bloodstains. The task will be made as revolting to his feelings as possible... After properly cleaning up his portion, the culprit will be immediately hanged."* The guilty men, of course, had fled long before Neill arrived. Neill proudly reported that *"a Mohammedan officer of our civil court, a great rascal"* had objected. He was flogged, and *"made to lick up part of the blood with his tongue."* Then, in Old Testament terms expressing the fanatical desire for vengeance which infected many British, Neill concluded: *"No doubt this is a strange law, but it suits the occasion well, and I hope I shall not be interfered with until the room is thoroughly cleansed in this way.... I will hold my own, with the help and the blessing of God. I cannot help seeing that His finger is in all this - we have been false to ourselves so often."*

Neill's ferocity was not exceptional. The British, enraged by the murder of their women and children in Cawnpore and elsewhere, were already responding with a reign of terror. By the middle of June, 1857, they had begun what one 19th-Century historian of the Mutiny, I.W. Kaye, called a *"Bloody Assize."* Indiscriminate lynchings were commonplace. *"Volunteer hanging parties,"* wrote Kaye, *"went out into the districts, and amateur executioners were not wanting to the occasion. One gentleman boasted of the numbers he had finished off quite 'in an artistic manner,' with mango trees for gibbets and elephants for drops, the victims of this wild justice being strung up, as though for pastime, in the form of figures of eight."*

Hanging, however, was usually thought too good for mutineers. When the facilities were available, it was usual to blow them from guns. It was claimed that this method contained *"two valuable elements of capital punishment; it was painless to the criminal and terrible to the beholder."* The ritual was certainly hideous. With great ceremony the victim was escorted to the parade ground while the band played some lively air. The victim's back was ranged against the muzzle of one of the big guns and he was strapped into position. Then the band would fall silent and the only sound would be the faint crackle of the portfire, as it was lowered to the touch-hole. With a flash and a roar, an obscene shower of blood and entrails would cover both the gunners and observers.

While Neill was engaged on his personal vengeance at Cawnpore, Havelock set out for Lucknow. He was, however, opposed not only by large bodies of mutineers, but also by heat-stroke and disease. Though he was victorious in a number of engagements, his troops were too weak to follow up their successes, and twice he was forced to fall back on Cawnpore. There he was able to regain sufficient strength to defeat, on August 16, a large force of mutineers who attempted to retake the city. But reinforcements arrived, and on September 19 Havelock was at last able to set out once again to relieve the long besieged people in the Lucknow Residency.

Inside the Residency, the garrison of 1,800 British men, women and children, as well as 1,200 native soldiers and non-combatants - had been holding out against a force of well over 20,000 Indian mutineers.

The siege had been precipitated by an ill-advised attempt by Sir Henry Lawrence to destroy a body of rebels at a place some ten miles from the Residency on June 29. The sortie had ended in a rout, and Lawrence had been compelled to retire on the Residency area before all his preparations there were complete. On the following day, he withdrew the garrison from the Machchi Bhawan, blowing up 240 barrels of gunpowder and five million rounds of ammunition when they left to keep these supplies from falling into the hands of the Indians.

The defence of the Residency was a nightmare. Because of Lawrence's refusal to demolish the mosques and houses surrounding the area, the defenders were under fire from the near-by roottops, suffering from what the military commander, Colonel Inglis, described as *"our very tenderness to the religious prejudices and respect to the rights of our rebellious citizens and soldiery."*

Casualties were high. The deadly sniper fire was soon supplemented by heavy artillery. On July I a shell burst in the room occupied by Lawrence. On being pressed to move to a safer place he replied that he *"did not believe that the enemy had an artilleryman good enough to put another shell into that small room."* He was wrong. About 8 a.m. the next day, while he lay exhausted on his bed, there was *"a sheet of flames and a terrific report."* To the cry from one of his aides, *"Sir Henry, are you hurt?"* he replied *"I am killed."* His pain dulled by chloroform, Lawrence survived for two days. In his conscious periods he dictated orders and requested that on his tomb should be placed the simple inscription: *"Here lies Henry Lawrence who tried to do his duty. May God have mercy on him."* In the night of July 4 he was buried with other dead in a large pit.

At least the men of the garrison had their duties. But the women and children were confined to the cellars, and lived a terrible, separate life punctuated only by alarms and deaths. Food was rationed, each person receiving *"attar or flour, which we made into chupatties; rice, dhal or peas; salt and meat."*

There were no proper cooking facilities so everything was cooked together, with ship's biscuits and some water, into a stew. *"But as the saucepan was of copper and could not be relined during tpe siege, the food when it was turned out was often perfectly green - hunger alone could make it enjoyable."* The children suffered most. The heat was intense and there were no coolies to pull the punkah fans. When the besiegers attacked the Residency, all the lights had to be put out and the children lay trembling in the darkness until the defenders had routed the Indians.

The rebels in Oudh had few military leaders of any quality, but among the civilians there was a woman of strong character and sense of purpose.

The Begum Hazrat Mahal, who had begun her career as adancing-girl, had caught the eye of the King of Oudh and borne him a son. After the rising in Oudh, the sepoys approached a number of the exKing's concubines. to persuade them to put up one of their 'sons as king. All refused until it came to the turn of Hazrat Mahal. She immediately agreed that her ten-year-old son, Birjis Qadr, should be proclaimed King and that she should be Regent during his minority. William Roward Russell - correspondent of the London Times - noted in his diary: *"This Begum exhibits great energy and ability.*

She has excited all Oudh to take up the interests of her sop, and the chiefs have sworn to be faithful to him."

A *"government"* was formed under Hazrat Mahal's authority and proclamations were made over the seal of King Birjis Qadr. The Begum toured through Oudh and was in constant correspondence with other leaders of the rebels. Little of this was known inside the Residency, for news was hard to come by. But a native spy was several times able to make his way through the rebel forces to Havelock's camp; and on September 23 a letter came from Sir James Outram, who had been sent to supersede Havelock but instead volunteered to serve under him until Lucknow was relieved.

In his letter Outram informed the commander of the garrison that the relieving force would be there in a few days.

On September 25, after bloody fighting, Havelock battered his way through to the Residency. *"The half-famished garrison,"* wrote Havelock, *"contrived to regale me, not only with beef cutlets, but with mock turtle soup and champagne."* But Havelock and Outram could do nothing in return. The force they had brought to Lucknow was not strong enough to break out again.

Reinforcements, however, were by now arriving in India in ever-increasing numbers. With them came two generals who were to bring the campaign against the mutineers to an end - Sir Colin Campbell and Sir Hugh Rose. On November 9, Campbell advanced with 5 ,000 men on Lucknow. To guide him, Outram sent Henry Kavanagh, who had volunteered to make his way through the rebel lines 'disguised as an Indian. It seemed a foolhardy enterprise, as he was nearly six feet tall, with red-gold hair and beard, and blazing blue eyes. But, made up with lampblack, he succeeded in reaching Campbell. On November 16, Campbell entered the city. He had moved slowly, careful not to risk unnecessary lives, but his caution - commendable in itself proved self-defeating because he allowed his enemy to escape time and again, and the campaign was prolonged.

Campbell slowly cleared the city of rebel forces as the garrison in the Residency made preparations for the evacuation. As the early darkness descended on November 19, the sad remnant of the garrison marched out. Campbell made no attempt to hold the city. He did not have the troops, and there were more pressing calls; at Cawnpore he had left General Windham with only 500 men to guard the one bridge by which mutineers fleeing from Lucknow might cross the River Ganges. Outram and Havelock were left, with 4,000 men, in a walled park four miles from Lucknow. There, weak with dysentery, Havelock waited for death. *"For 40 years,"* he told Outram, *"I have so endeavoured to rule my life that when death came I might face it without fear."* It came on the morning of November 24.

Campbell's weary men hurried towards Cawnpore, hampered by the women and children who were refugees from Lucknow. Windham, faced by a rebel force of some 20,000 men under the command of the best of the rebel generals, Tantia Topi, reluctantly had had to give ground. But with Campbell's arrival, the British took the offensive, routed Tantia Topi and saved Cawnpore.

The campaign was by no means over. It was three months before Campbell could retake Lucknow in March 1858, and it was not until May, with the successful action at Bareilly in Rohilkhand, that large-scale operations in the north came to an end.

The fall of the two great centres of the revolt, Delhi and Lucknow, marked the beginning of the end, and many mutineers realized it. The civilian leaders of the Mutiny disappeared, some never to be heard of again.

Those who had taken advantage of the breakdown of British rule to payoff old scores or acquire an easy fortune faded into the background from which they had emerged. Only a few, like the Rani of Jhansi and Tantia Topi, fought on to the end alongside their sepoy followers who - as the

British had made clear - stood as much chance of death if they surrendered as if they went on fighting to the bitter end.

While Campbell completed his campaign in Oudh, Sir Henry Rose turned on the rebels in central India.

The End Game

Rose, starting from Bornbay, made for Jhansi, which he reached on March 21. Before he could besiege the citadel, he had to march out against Tantia Topi, who had recovered from his defeat by Campbell. Once more the Indian was defeated and Rose could return to the storming of Jhansi. Even though the British guns had continued to bombard the city while Rose was away dealing with Tantia Topi, it still looked formidable. The great fort seemed untouched and the Rani's flag still flew defiantly from one of the towers. This remarkable woman, only 23 years old, had been a reluctant rebel. She took up arms after the British accused her of leading a massacre of white women and children. Although there is no evidence of her complicity in the deed, she was condemned by the British as the "Jezebel of India" and chose to fight. But without hoped for support from Tantia Topi, the plight of the city was serious.

When the British launched their assault, they were met with strong resistance but finally broke through the walls into the city. No quarter was given by the British, even to women and children. Those of the rebels who could not escape, wrote an eyewitness, "threw their women and babes down wells and then jumped down themselves."

The fighting went on for some days, until the streets were so full of corpses that all the squares were turned into cremation grounds and *"it became difficult to breathe, as the air stank with the odour of burning human flesh and the stench of rotting animals in the streets."* The British claimed to have killed 5,000 *"rebels"* in the town, but many must have been innocent citizens.

The Rani was not among the dead. On April 4, she and a small party had left the fort and made for the north gate of the city. Passing through, she avoided Rose's patrols and was many miles away before the British discovered she had gone.

A cavalry detachment, sent in pursuit, caught up with the party, and according to some sources the British officer commanding was wounded in a sword-fight by the Rani herself. The Rani and four retainers reached the town of Kalpi the next day, and were joined there by Tantia Topi. Rallying their forces, they descended on Gwalior, an immense fortress held by a ruler loyal to the British. The ruler marched out against the rebels, but his army deserted to them and he himself barely escaped capture.

Rose and his exhausted troops took Gwalior on June 20. Among those who fell in the fighting was the Rani of Jhansi, dressed as a man, her great jewelled sword still in her hand. Tantia Topi escaped, only to be betrayed to the British; he was hanged in April, 1859.

Peace in India was not officially declared until July 8, 1859. *"War is at an end; Rebellion is put down; the Noise of Arms is no longer heard where the enemies of the State have persisted in their last Struggle;' the Presence of large Forces in the Field has ceased to be necessary; Order is re-established; and peaceful Pursuits have everywhere been resumed."* So ran Lord Canning's proclamation. The British in the subcontinent and at home began to breathe freely once again.

Legacy of the Mutiny

There had been no real danger that British rule in India would be overthrown. The majority of the native soldiers had remained loyal. In fact, without them the British could hardly have suppressed the rebellion. During the attack on Delhi, for example, of 11,200 combatants on the British side no fewer than 7,900 had been Indian. Large areas of the country remained unruffled by what the Indians called *"the devil's wind."*

Though the British lost at most about 11,000 men, three-quarters of them killed by disease or heat-stroke, the overall cost was high. There are no reliable figures for sepoy or civilian deaths, but many thousands, both guilty and innocent, had perished. The scars of the rebellion were there for all to see. Ruined cities, burnt villages and dead fields ran like a swathe across northern India. The country was further burdened by a debt of £30,000,000 and all the problems of reconstruction. In Britain, the Mutiny did more than produce a wave of hysteria and a desire for vengeance: it convinced the politicians that the British Crown must assume full responsibility from the East India Company for the government of India. This was done by Royal proclamation on November 1, 1858.

One of the first problems which had to be tackled was the reorganization of the army. The Company's white troops were disbanded (and some of those men mutinied in protest). Henceforth there was to be a permanent garrison of British Army troops serving only in India. Regiments of the Queen's forces would do tours of duty and then be replaced. The problem of the Indian element in the army was much more difficult. But two innovations were essential: the proportion of native to British troops was not to be allowed to exceed two to one, and the artillery was to be almost exclusively in the hands of the Queen's regiments. In the Bengal Army, the number of native infantry regiments was reduced from 146 in 1857 to 72, and similar reductions took place in the Bombay and Madras armies. The number of men in each regiment was also reduced to 600. By 1861, there were about 70,000 British troops to 135,000 native troops, and the British held all the arsenals and the principal forts.

The main task of civil reconstruction took many years. The first step was an attempt at reconciliation. The princes, who had generally either sided with the British or had been peutral, were no longer threatened with annexation.

Over the years that followed the Mutiny, every attempt was made to show them that their true interests lay with the British, and everything was done to give them a position - albeit empty of real power in the new Empire of India. Recognizing that one of the causes of the Mutiny had been the fear that the British intended to make all Indians Christians, Queen Victoria proclaimed that although *"firmly relying ourselves upon the truth of Christianity and acknowledging with gratitude the solace of religion, we disclaim alike the right and the desire to impose our convictions on any other subjects."*

Only one of the rebel leaders replied to the Queen's proclamation. The Begum Hazrat Mahal of Oudh, refusing the offer of a pardon and a pension stayed in Nepal, to which she had escaped, and from there issued her reply. The Begum's *"proclamation"* is an unusual document. It dissected Queen Victoria's text, paragraph by paragraph, and in its way it enshrines the fears and misunderstandings that led to the sepoy revolt. Her criticism of the clause guaranteeing freedom of religious worship is worth quoting, for behind it lies the truth of the tragedy of 1857:

"In the proclamation it is written that the Christian religion is true, but no other creed will suffer oppression, and that the laws will be observed towards all. What has the administration of justice to do with the truth or falsehood of a religion? That religion is true which acknowledges one God and knows no other. Where there are three gods in a religion, neither Mussulman nor Hindus - nay, not even Jews, sun-worshippers or fire-worshippers - can believe it to be true. To eat pigs and drink wine, to bite greased cartridges, and to mix pig's fat with flour and sweetmeats, to destroy Hindu and Mussulman temples on pretence of making roads, to build churches, to send clergymen into the streets and alleys to preach the Christian religion, to institute English schools, and pay people a monthly stipend for learning the English Sciences, while the places of worship of Hindu and Mussulman are to this day neglected - with all this how can the people believe that religion will not be interfered with? The rebellion began with religion,

and for it millions of men have been killed. Let not our subjects be deceived; thousands were deprived of their religion in the northwest and thousands were hanged rather than abandon their religion."

What, then, had the revolt been? Was it merely a military mutiny in a part of the army, as the British believed, or a national uprising, as later Indian historians have argued? The truth lies somewhere in between. It was traditional India that had risen against the British, the India which remembered its past, hated the present and dreaded the future that was now absolutely certain to belong to the Westernized Indian, and not to the Indian soldiers or princes.

Beyond Mangal Pandey: 1857 Was John Company's Intelligence Rout

A hundred years after the 1757 coup d'etat in Murshidabad, the formidable British intelligence-gathering system had collapsed. The 1757 coup was executed with such perfection by Robert Clive that it enabled the East India Company to acquire the *diwani* of Bengal, Bihar and Odisha.

But the collapse was palpable. When a nascent mutiny plot in Barrackpore was exposed by sepoy Mangal Pandey (of the 34th Bengal Native Infantry) in a drug-hazed stupor, the British failed to detect the rumblings that would take most of north India by storm. The onset of the 1857 mutiny has been interpreted by historians of all shades as the first war of independence, a peasant-and-elite backlash against the underhand means employed to take over Awadh. Widely considered to have begun with the shots fired by (sepoy No. 1446) Pandey at his British superiors on the parade grounds of the Barrackpore cantonment on March 29 afternoon, the mutiny has also been interpreted as a violent reaction to the loss of sepoys' privileges and even the centrality of religion and caste.

Pandey's rebellious act was followed by a two-day court martial which ordered that he be hanged. The ruling was duly carried out on 8 April in the gallows of Barrackpore cantonment. A few days later, his uncle Issuri Prasad was also hanged for complicity.

Neither a Martyr Nor a Hero

Pandey's martyrdom has been questioned by the foremost 1857 historian, Rudrangshu Mukherjee, for whom "There is no evidence to justify the view that this sepoy was a martyr and hero who decided to die with honor, betraying none of his co-conspirators, and expressing no regret or remorse." It is Mukherjee's case – and rightly so – that there was no causal relationship between Pandey's solo rebellion and the more concerted action of the sepoys in Meerut.

While it is certain that Pandey "had no notion of patriotism or even of India," he appeared to have been fired by two factors: the imminent arrival of the 19th regiment of the 34th BNI to Barrackpore for disbandment (for refusing to use the so-called greased cartridges) and some bare knowledge that something violent was brewing in the sepoys' barracks. The British failed to read the cryptic messages in Pandey's invective-peppered outburst.

Intelligence Failure

What is more important than Pandey's motive and agency is the British failure to read the sepoys' minds across north India's different cantonments where they rose once the mutiny broke out in Meerut on 10 May 1857.

In his compelling argument, CA Bayly says that the "dramatic onset of the Rebellion of 1857" was an "acute failure" of British intelligence gathering and analysis, especially after the informational success achieved in their campaign against *thugees* and other criminal conspiracies through the first four decades of the 19th century.

Bayly suggests that by the 1840s and 1850s, East India Company officials in northern India had eschewed human intelligence, gathered by "resourceful *harkaras* and influential *munshis*" and had begun to rely more on statistical surveys, court papers and the vernacular press. The new generation of young military officers were "ignorant" and "found it more difficult to communicate" with the older generation of Indian "subalterns" or non-commissioned officers in the employ of John Company. It was the yawning difference and disconnect between officers and soldiers that left the British high and dry on the intelligence front.

Inability to Interpret Messages

"By the 1850s, Anglo-Indian society was more isolated and obsessed with events in England", as military officers stationed in northern India struggled to come to grip with "Indian mentalities".

As Bayly writes, "The inability of officials and soldiers to interpret or respond to the messages of unease which came in from so many sources during the 1850s was at least as important as the lack of accurate intelligence."

While the massive failures of intelligence was the outcome of "two generations of social disruption and official insensitivity", the British must be credited with responding to failure by quickly taking counter-measures, even as they and the insurgent sepoys struggled to take control of the telegraph wires which at the time was the fastest means of communication over hundreds of miles.

Mastery Over Telegraph Wires

It was the British military's quick recovery from the great failure of January-May 1857 and subsequent near-complete mastery over the telegraph wires, though belated, coupled with postal surveillance, that prevented its rout on the scattered battlefields across the Gangetic plains.

But like every failure and lessons learnt from them, the 1857 conflagration, which dragged into 1859 in some parts of north India, threw up important institutional changes even as the old order perished. First, the suppression of the great uprising led to the quick demise of the East India Company as the Indian dominion passed to the British crown.

Second, the British in India, now acting under and governed by the crown, but under stricter watch of their parliament, institutionalised police operations by codifying crime and punishment in the shape of the Indian Penal Code of 1860. Sedition was a key provision.

But, nearly 160 years after the great uprising, when democracy runs across the length and breadth of the country, why must the sedition law survive?

6

Mangal Pandey: The Man Behind Revolt

We read, see and analyse history in different angles. So is the case of India's First War of Independence or The Revolt of 1857. For Indians it is the First War of Indian Independence but for British it is a Sepoy Mutiny.

However, the First War of Independence happened because of a brave son of India, Mangal Pandey. It was this man who woke-up the Indian masses from sleep to fight for the nation, which was ailing under the British. Mangal Pandey was the torch-bearer.

The rising was, literally, triggered by a gun, the Pattern 1853 Enfield rifled musket. To load the new rifle, soldiers had to bite the cartridge, open and pour the gunpowder into the rifle's muzzle, then stuff the cartridge case, which was coated with some kind of grease to make it waterproof, into the musket as wadding, before loading it with a ball.

A rumour spread that the cartridges were greased with lard (pork fat) which was regarded as unclean by Muslims, or tallow (beef fat), regarded as sacred to Hindus. At that time it was believed that a high-caste Hindu who ate cows' flesh would lose caste, with dreadful consequences both in the present life and the next. Slowly discontent was rising which ultimately lead to the revolt.

On March 29, 1857 at the Barrackpore (now Barrackpur) near Calcutta, Mangal Pandey attacked and injured his British sergeant on the parade ground and wounded an Adjutant with a sword after failing to shoot at him. The officer in charge General Hearsay ordered a Jamadaar of the troops, a man called Ishwaria Pandey to arrest Mangal. But he refused. The whole regiment drew back from restraining or arresting Mangal.

Failing to incite the spirit of nationalism in his comardes Mangal tried to end his life. He turned the gun against himself and used his foot to try to pull the trigger to shoot himself. But Mangal failed and was captured. He was court-martialed on April 6 and was hanged at Barrackpore on April 8, 1857.

His execution was actually scheduled for April 18. But was carried out ten days earlier.

Because the Britishers feared the possibility of a massive revolt. As a collective punishment for his act, the entire regiment was also dismissed. This was the end of the first warrior of Indian Independence.

As per the records he joined the British East India Company in 1849 at the age of 22. Mangal was a part of the 5th Company of the 34th BNI regiment. Little is known of his life before the momentous war of Independence but he has been declared a martyr since. On March 29, 1857 Mangal Pandey reaped the seed for a struggle which gave India her freedom and us Indians independence.

The Government of India commemorated Mangal Pandey by issuing a postage stamp bearing his image on October 5,

1984. A film based on his life and times titled Mangal Pandey: The Rising starring Indian actor, Aamir Khan directed by Ketan Mehta was released in August 2005.

The life of Mangal Pandey was also the subject of a stage play titled The Roti Rebellion, which was written and directed by Supriya Karunakaran. The play was organized by Sparsh, a theatre group and presented in June 2005.

Man Who Led the Mutiny

Amaresh Misra records the life and times of the revolutionary Mangal Pandey, who triggered the First War of Independence.

Date: March 29, 1857—place: Barrackpore in the Bengal division. *"The 34th BNI had a British Sergeant Major, Hewson by name, attached to it, and he was told that a sepoy by the name of Mangal Pandey had come out of the lines with his musket loaded, which was against standing orders. In turn he informed the adjutant Lieutenant Baugh. Hewson and Baugh found Mangal Pandey outside the quarter guard calling on his comrades to help him strike a blow for their religion: he fired at Baugh and brought down his horse, and then took on both Hewson and Baugh with his tulwar and was a match for them both. The Sepoy was clearly under the influence of some drug, although he was previously of good character. The guard of twenty sepoys looked on unconcerned, only one Sheikh Paltu, came to the aid of the Europeans and held Mangal Pandey while they escaped. Colonel Wheeler of the 34th came up and ordered the guard to arrest the mutineer but no one obeyed him. Similarly Brigadier Grant came up and was ignored. Mangal Pandey was continuing to taunt his comrades. Hearsey and his two sons then rode up and Hearsey with some courage threatened the guard with his revolver and forced them to move against the mutineer, but the latter turned his musket against himself: he fell wounded and was arrested and taken off to the hospital."*

Thus began the saga of Mangal Pandey, then the first mutineer, now the first hero of the first war of Indian Independence. Who was he? What were his motivations?

Who were the British officers whose names appear in records and history? What was their relation to the man? Was Mangal Pandey a conscious revolutionary or actually acting under the impulse of some drug? What were the conditions that produced a character like him? Was he linked to earlier and latter events? Was he part of a wider conspiracy of acting alone? What implications did the Mangal Pandey incident really have on the wider uprising that took place in May that year, an uprising that shook the foundations of the greatest Empire of the day?

Hundred and forty eight years after the Barrackpore incident when India is close to celebrating the 150th anniversary of the event, these questions remain at best an enigma. The fact of the matter is that India knows very little about her first hero. Documents are scarce and mention only the outlines; the Indian literary world, and books on 1857, have ignored him; there is a major dispute about his place of birth and origin; and it is only now that a film has been made.

The British came as traders; their new army was part of the East India Company. It tapped the enormous market of martial people in the Awadh and east UP region. Company soldiers were called Sepoys—they were given tight jackets, tunics and pants to wear in the European style. Overnight Tulsidas followers were turned into members of semi-European regiments.

The change was as a dramatic as it was singular. Brahmins had been part of the cavalry dominated Mughal armies. But these armies had a roving nature—tied to Mansabdars or the military-administrative elite they were nevertheless fluid moving from one Commander to the to other. The Mughals had created a largely city oriented professional army—the British Sepoys were part of a professional peasant army.

Mangal Pandey's village society was in a state of acute flux—his own Sepoy world was crumbling. He was a Brahmin of Awadh who had to set things right even if it meant revolt.

Mangal Pandey was born in Faizabad's Akbarpur Tehsil. The latter were British administrative divisions borrowed from post-Mughal Indian administrative lingo—they symbolized the level immediately below the zillah (district). The date, as recorded in shattered pages of documents still retained by surviving members of his clan, was presumably July 19, 1827'85.

The village in which young Mangal opened his eyes was Surhurpur—a small sleepy hamlet, which still retains the dusty rustic look, that speck of golden grime, the wont of Awadh, distinguishing the region from the more greener pastures of east UP. Divakar Pandey, Mangal's father actually belonged to another village – Dugvaan-Rahimpur in Faizabad Tehsil. He had settled in Surhurpur as his father-in-law had no male heir – the village property therefore was bequeathed to the son-in-law.

Mangal Pandey entered the east India Company Bengal army in 1849. He was 22, a tall lad, lean and well built. Village anecdotes paint him as a man 9 feet tall—this excusable exaggeration however conceals the truth. The peasants recruited by the Company as Sepoys were mostly unusually tall—so much so that during the 1857 wars Scot Highlanders were brought over especially from Britain to match Sepoy strength and height. Local perceptions played a great part in victory or defeat—the natives considered Sepoys invincible.

The 1806 Vellore Mutiny by the Madras army was threatening—it followed a pattern similar to 1857. Sepoy resentment rose first over interference in wearing caste marks—soon Tipu Sultan sons, captive in Vellore fort were declared rulers as Madras Sepoys went on rampage killing their officers and liberating their environs.

Bloodthirsty force was used to quell the Vellore mutiny—then Barrackpore, the scene of Mangal Pandey's defiance faced a serious crisis in 1824-25. Sepoys in their hundreds shot in the air, killed a section of their officers and deserted en masse.

The British began to see the Bengal army as a mess and Sepoys as spoiled children. There was politics behind this paternalism—ostensibly the disputes were over pay and other allowances given to the Sepoys before but slowly being curtailed by the British.

Brahminism was a threat because the British wanted to follow the Goa pattern. Here high caste Hindus had converted to Christianity and the old status quo had merged into a new religion creating an effective base for the Portuguese administration. The British wanted Brahmins as partners—making them the administrative equivalents of the comprador traders and bourgeoisie.

In Mangal's personal story, the Aalha speaks about his break up with Nakki Khan sometime in late 1856. The involvement of a girl is vaguely mentioned but then the friends are shown as patching up—the major fall out seems to have occurred when Nakki Khan informed Mangal of new thoughts blowing in the wind.

Apparently Nakki, who had become a Sufi as well, had come fresh from a religious fair where he had heard Hindu and Muslim saints venting anger at British rule, spelling out its doom in 1857, exactly hundred years after the battle of Plassey.

Mangal Pandey is probably the missing link that connected mutinies in Behrampore and Barrackpore. He was the active who much in the tradition of martyrs decided to sacrifice his life in order to rouse the masses. The Aalha speaks of Nakki Khan and Mangal visiting Calcutta, taking a dip in the holy Ganges and swearing to root out foreign rule. The next stop Mangal made was at a Calcutta mansion to bid goodbye to a Hindustani ladylove married to a Bengali clerk, smarting under colonial Indian male chauvinism. Nakki Khan stood on the doorway looking out for possible intruders as Mangal drank *Bhang* and made love. He was a long distance away from home and he was soon going to die.

The Uprising

Ever since the victory of Plassey in 1757 AD, and putting the French East India Company to its political doom, the British East India Company established its rule in Indian and gradually tightened its grip over the major part of the country. The British introduced significant changes in thedifferent spheres, which proved disastrous to the solidarity of their rule. The rival forces joined their hands, thus leading to the great upheaval in 1857 AD.

Divergent views are held on the nature of the 1857 uprising, whether it was a military mutiny or the first national war of independence, or a Hindu-Muslim voice against the impending danger of Christianity-is a matter of controversy among the historians. Sir John Lawrence and James Seeley feel that the uprising of 1857 was a "wholly unpatriotic and selfish Sepoy Mutiny with no native leadership and no popular support." This opinion is accepted by Trevelyan, C. Raikes, P. E. Roberts, and Edwards and Garratt. The contention of these writers is that the uprising was influenced by the sepoys, who had their own grievances and held the British government responsible for the same. The revolt had started from the cantonments and remained effective around the same. Obviously, it was the case of greased cartridges which sparked the fire. On the other hand, the civilians, by and large, remained unaffected by all these developments. Indeed, the Indian rulers, who had grievances against the British, rose to the occasion after the sepoy uprising; otherwise they had no courage to take such a step.

Kaye and Malleson name it an organised Hindu-Muslim rising, which Reese prefers to call it a war of religious fanaticism against Christianity. J. Outram is of the opinion that "it was a Mohammedan conspiracy making capital of Hindu grievances." However, Benjamin Disraeli observes that it was a well-planned, well-organised and vigilant event.

There is a nationalist approach to this event, forwarded by V.D. Savarkar, K.M. Panikkar and Ashok Mehta, who observe that it was the First National War of Independence, in which Indian masses from all walks of life participated. The grievances of the people, as a consequence of one hundred yeas of British rule, forced them to stand in unison, putting aside all their differences, as matters caste and religion. The evidence came when even the Hindus acknowledged Bahadur Shah II as their ruler. The Hindus and the Muslims swore by the Ganges and the Holy Quran to get rid of the British rule, which was the common objective of the rebels everywhere. The event was confined not only to the military Mutiny, but spread rapidly and achieved the character of "a popular rebellion and a war of Indian Independence."

After going through the above analysis, one comes to certain conclusions:

(a) It was a military mutiny.

(b) It was a religious war of the Hindus and the Muslims against Christianity.

(c) It was a national war of independence aimed at the freedom from the alien rule, and in which Indians from all walks of life participated.

However, there are certain limitations in accepting any of these views. In fact, the movement was never religious in character. Christianity was being supported by the British government, which was posing a general threat to the Hinduism and the Islam. But in this struggle those who were defeated were the followers of a religion and not religion itself. Secondly, it was not on the whole, a sepoy mutiny. Though the sepoys provided boon to other elements to operate, they did not take part in it from all over the country. In many places, many of them even supported the British cause. Thirdly, the revolt did not cover the whole of the country, but its scope was limited only to certain parts. The majority of the North and the Deccan remained entirely unaffected or fought on the side of the foreigners against the rebels.

The revolt had nothing constructive as its objective rather than the anti-British base. There is a recent approach towards the character of the mutiny, led by Dr. R.C Majumdar. He holds the view that "the so called First National War of Independence of 1857 is neither first nor National, nor a War of Independence." According to him, those who participated did so not out of any nationalist consideration, but only to further their self-interests.

In fact, the population was, by and large, unaware of nationalism during 1857. The struggle was much less for the freedom of India, but for Jhansi or Oudh etc. It is the general contention that the civilians also participated in the revolt along with the sepoys, and that the former were punished to death in great number because of this reason. But it is significant to understand the social stratification of the civilians in this uprising.

The major role in the rural areas was played by the peasant, who held the moneylenders as the source of their agony. These moneylenders were supported by the British which caused unrest among the peasants against the government. However, the revolt was strong in the rural areas only where the moneylenders' position was weak and the hereditary caste and clan groups were strong. There were certain castes and tribes in the Central and Northern India, which had been subdued, found an opportunity when the British rule was shaken. They again returned to their traditional profession of loot and plunder, and there was nothing national in it. As matters the feudal lords, they had an intention of regaining their old status of the medieval times.

From the above survey, it is not proper to name this event

either the military uprising, because it remained active in and around the cantonments; or the first war of independence, because people from all walks of life took active part in it without any distinction of caste or religion. People lacked the sense of national consciousness, and those who rebelled did so influenced by a variety of grievances. The revolt, however, sowed the seeds of national awakening, which were to be observed in the coming years.

The major reason regarding the outbreak of the revolt is associated with the greased cartridge controversy. The soldiers were provided with the new Enfield Rifles and the cartridges were allegedly greased with the fat of cow and pig. These cartridges were to be opened with the mouth before using in the rifles. It enraged the Hindus and the Muslim soldiers, because it hurt their religious sentiments. When the soldiers objected to its use, they were court-martialled, thus "falling as a spark on dry tinder." However, the cartridge issue was not the whole important. Obviously, it had only enraged the soldiers and gave the military feed to the discontented general masses and the ruling classes, who hated the British rule for its political, economic, socio-religious and military policies. In fact, "the first century of British rule in India set the stage for the great tragic drama which was to celebrate the centenary of its foundation in the blood and tears."

The British came to India as traders and took advantage of its political weaknesses, created by its lack of unity and mutual distrust. As a consequence of the French defeats in the Carnatic Wars, and the British victories at Plassey (1757) and Buxar (1764), the East India Company established its rule in Bengal. Apart from defeating the Marathas and the Mysore, the British made a successful bid to hold their political control over different States in India. The Subsidiary Alliance System, formed by Lord Wellesley, set up the British influence in many States including Oudh, Tanjore, Carnatic, Hyderabad, Mysore, Nagpur, Indore, Gwalior, Baroda, Jaipur, Jodhpur and Bhopal, and annexed many parts into the Company's Empire.

The work of the political conquests was carried on by Lord Hastings, William Bentick and Ellenborough. The crises reached its climax under Lord Dalhousie. The Doctrine of Lapse gave the authority to the Company Empire to annex all the States of the heirless rulers. The adopted sons of such rulers could not succeed unless permitted by the East India Company. Luckily or otherwise, the States of Satara, Jhansi, Nagpur, Jaitpur, Sambalpur, Udaipur and Bhagalpur fell a prey to this policy which caused restlessness among the ruling classes. The titles and pensions of the Raja of Tanjore, the Nawab of Carnatic and Nana Sahib, the adopted son of Peshwa Baji Rao II were abolished. Dalhousie's imperialism crossed all the limits, when in 1856, Oudh was annexed to the Company's rule on the pretext of mal-administration. Even the Mughal Emperor, Bahadur Shah II, was informed that his sons would be deprived of the title, fort and palace, which hurt the Muslim sentiments in the country and added fuel to the fire. The Mughal Empire was, in fact, looked upon as the pillar of Islamic State in India and the loss of the Empire was, in other terms, a loss to the position of the Muslims.

The administrative set up was also a cause of discontentment to the Indians. The British ruled the country from England. They had no sentiments, and no sense of gratitude for the Indians. The natives were deprived of the high posts in the administration. Though the Charter Act of 1833 mentioned that caste, creed or colour would not become a barrier to appointments, it was not implemented. No doubt, Lord William Bentick had appointed Indians on lower posts, but the key posts were reserved for the Europeans.

The Charter Act of 1853, recommended for the competitive examinations for those aspiring to higher administrative positions, but the Indians found its terms too harsh for themselves to get through. The examinations were conducted in England, and the maximum age limit was 22 years. The highest office any Indian could aspire for, was that of a Deputy Collector in the Executive and a Sadar Amin in the Judiciary. The natives could not approach their English officers easily, and were ill-treated by them. They were considered inferior "even to the backward persons of the most backward of the European countries." Sir Syed Ahmed Khan exposed in The Causes of the Indian Revolt that the absence of Indian representatives in the Governor-General's Legislative Council was an important factor leading to the revolt. The Government could not understand the feeling of the subjects. In his opinion, it was in the general interest of the government to have the representative voice in its Council.

Suspicions and hatred towards the British rule increased on the socio-religious grounds. The government allowed the Christian Missionaries in 1813 to spread their religion in India, and they did so with much zeal. Even the government supported their cause. Missionary schools were opened with this very object. During a severe famine in 1837 in Upper India, the relief work was left with the charitable institutions, and it gave an opportunity to the missionaries to undertake their proselytizing task. Those who converted to Christianity were fed properly. The Disabilities Act of 1856 guaranteed the rights over inheritance, even after conversion, but only to Christianity.

The spread of Western education, the introduction of female education and the establishment of railways and telegraph system were looked upon by the Indians an instrument to crush their religion. They government also started interfering into the social structure of the Indians. The abolition of Sati and female infanticide, and the introduction of secular legal system was a danger to the prevailing structure.

The abolition of Persian in the courts also offended the Muslims. The new system affected the priestly classes to a large extent and they toyed with the fears of the common masses in instigating them against the government.

Here the blame rests not with the common masses, as they were ignorant of the objectives and utilization of all these innovations, but with the officials themselves. They issued certain statements, which raised the fears in the minds of the natives. Mangles, the Chairman of the Board of Directors, declared in the House of Commons, "Providence had entrusted the extensive Empire of Hindustan to England in order that the banner of Christ should wave triumphant from one end of India to the other. Every one must exert all his strength—in continuing in the country the grand work of making all Indians Christians." The statement of Major Edwards that "the Christianization of India was to be the ultimate end of our continued possession of it," made the Indians deadly against the British rule.

The British officials, military as well as civil, used abusive language for Lord Rama and the Prophet, and prevailed upon their subordinates to convert to Christianity. The Indians were discriminated even in the courts where they were meted out harsh punishments even for minor crimes, while the Christians received mild punishments for complex crimes.

The economic policies of the British had grave consequences on the Indian public, which stood to revolt. The economic exploitation of India started since the British established their rule here. The British economic policy proved beneficial to England, while it had drastic results over India. The Indian trade was kept in the hands of the British traders and were given many concessions, which had a negative impact on the economy of Indian traders.

The Charter Act of 1813 brought to an end the monopoly of the East India Company to trade with India, while the Company rule began to serve the commercial interests of the English traders and the industrialists. To start with, the British opened their trade in spices, cotton, etc. but after the industrial revolution their policy in trade matters also changed. "India became a milch cow, while her own sons were gradually pushed to the starvation wage." India exported raw materials to England at cheap rates, while became a ready market for the sale of finished goods at high prices. The government aimed at destroying the Indian trade and manufactures; therefore it imposed heavy custom duties on Indian made goods in England, while a nominal duty was imposed on British manufactures in India. The result was that India became an economic colony for the British.

Not only were the trade and industry of India destroyed, but also the British rule led to the deterioration of agriculture. The revenue policy of the British did no favour either to the peasants or the zamindars. Revenue was imposed on the rent-free lands given in the form of religious grants as well. To make the matters worse, Lord William Bentick had confiscated land from a number of landlords who could not prove that these were assigned to their forefathers by the then rulers.

The army's role in the revolt was very significant, but the soldiers had their own grievances. The inequality in the status of the Indians and European soldiers was disliked by the Indian troops. All the commissioned ranks were reserved for the Europeans, and the highest rank in the army an Indian could aspire for was that of a Subedar with a salary of Rs. 60 per month. However, their European counterparts used to draw the salary 7 to 8 times more than the Indians. The additional bhattas (allowances) of the soldiers was also stopped. The efforts of the British Generals to propagate Christianity among their ranks, was also a cause of misery to the Indian mercenaries. The number of the Indian soldiers in the army was much larger as compared to the Europeans. The heavy losses that the British had to suffer in Afghanistan encouraged the Indian soldiers. Discipline among them was waning and Lord Dalhousie had informed the authorities in England about it. To make the matters worse, the soldiers were abandoned to send the revenue free letter according to the Post Office Act, 1854. They had been enjoying this privilege so far. The General Services Recruitment Act, 1856, required the new recruits to serve any part they were sent. Though the new Act did not affect the old incumbents, it became very unpopular, because service in the Bengal Army was almost hereditary. It was felt against the social and religious beliefs to go across the sea. Earlier too, the Barrackpore Regiment was disbanded in 1824, when the soldiers had refused to go to Burma.

In the meantime, the controversy regarding the greased cartridges caught much fire, ultimately leading to the mutiny. Soon, it spread among the civilians as well, who were waiting for an opportune moment to strike.

The banner of revolt was raised at Barrackpore on March 29, 1857. A young Brahmin sepoy Mangal Pandey, refused to use the greased cartridges and killed his European officers. The government disbanded the 34 N.I. Regiment and punished the guilty rebels. The mutiny spread like wild fire and in May 1857, 85 sepoys of 3rd Cavalry Regiment, at Meerut, were court-martialled on their refusal to use the cartridges. On May 10, the rebels killed many European officers and got their fellows released. Even General Hewlett, at the command of 2200 soldiers, could not dare resist the mutineers.

On May 12, the rebels attacked Delhi. Lt. Willough by surrendered after putting some resistance. Bahadur Shah Zafar was declared the Emperor of India, to which he hesitantly accepted. The loss of Delhi was very tragic to the British position. Soon the rebellion centred around Lucknow, Kanpur, Barreily, Benaras, Jhansi and many towns in the Central and Northern India. To crush the revolt, Lord Canning felt the expediency of re-establishing the British authority over Delhi. Military assistance was sought from the Presidencies of Bombay and Madras and the Chief Commissioner of Punjab Sir, John Lawrence. The British got valuable services from the Gorkhas, the Sikhs and a number of rulers from the Indian states. Delhi was besieged under Sir Henry Bernard and Wilson, while the rebels fought bravely under Mirza Mughal and Bakht Khan. However, General Nicolson succeeded in recapturing Delhi on September 14, but soon after succumbed to his injuries received during the battle. Bahadur Shah was arrested from the tomb of Humayun by Lt. Hudson, while his two sons and a grandson were publicly shot. The loot and plunder of Delhi by the British troops continued for three days and surpassed even the loot of Nadir Shah.

The revolt broke out in Lucknow on June 4, 1857. The rebels attacked the British Residency and killed its Resident, Sir Henry Lawrence. The efforts of Havelock and Outram to recover Lucknow failed. Later on Sir Colin Campbell at the head of the Gorkha Regiment, entered the city in March 1858, but the guerilla activities continued till September.

In June 1857, the revolt broke out in Kanpur also and the rebellious troops occupied the city. Nana Sahib declared himself the Peshwa and forced Sir Hugh Wheeler to surrender on June 27. Taking revenge of the atrocities committed on the Indians by General Neil at Allahabad and Benaras, the Indian troops murdered many English men and women in Kanpur.

The decisive battle was fought in the first week of December, when Sir Colin Campbell defeated the rebels on December 6. Nana Sahib fled towards Nepal, while Tantia Tope escaped and joined Lakshmibai, the queen of Jhansi. Lakshmibai, the widow of King Gangadhar Rao, led the rebels in Jhansi in June 1857. On April 3, 1858, Sir Hugh Rose attacked Jhansi and recaptured it. Lakshmibai fled to Kalpi, where assisted by Tantia Tope, inflicted many losses on the enemies. Ultimately, the British defeated the rebels on May 24. Lakshmibai and Tantia Tope fled to Gwalior and sought Sicindia's help. But Sicindia, showing loyalty to the British refused to assist them. However, the troops of Gwalior revolted against Scindia and forced him to flee towards Agra. Sir Hugh Rose attacked Gwalior on June 11, and after a fierce battle of 8 days, captured the town Rani Lakshmibai gave a fine expression of her bravery, but died on the battlefield. Tantia Tope, who had fled to the South, was arrested in April 1859.

The death of Lakshmibai proved to be a death knell to the revolt. Though there were rebellions in Rohilkhand, Bareilly, Shahjahanpur, Bihar, parts of Rajputana, and the Maratha territories, these had no impression on the destruction of the alien rule and were very easily crushed. By December 1858, the British were able to re-establish their authority all over India.

The rebels had shown the signs of their extreme bravery, but the British had their day. Varieties of factors are held responsible for the failure of this upheaval from the Indian point of view. The superiority of the British arms, discipline in their troops and their control over telegraph system played a very significant role in the Company's success over the rebels. At this critical juncture, the British secured valuable support from many Indian States including Patiala, Jind, Nabha, Kapurthala, Gwalior, Hyderabad, Rampur etc. Even Canning observed that the British would have been forced to pack, had Scindia joined the rebels.

The political diplomacy of the British had its own role in this success. They created the communal differences among the Hindus, the Muslims and the Sikhs to a great extent and successfully played on these. On the other hand, they won the support from the rulers of the States. In his analysis, Dr. R. C. Majumdar observes, "A race which could successfully employ the sepoys against the Sikhs, and then the Sikhs against the sepoys, the sepoys against the Pathans and the Gurkhas, and then the Pathans and the Gurkhas against the sepoys, certainly deserves a Empire." A serious drawback on the part of the rebels, was the lack of any common solid objective. Apart from their limited resources, indeed, the rebels had an anti-British attitude in common, but they had nothing national in them. Each party had its divergent interests and had only to fulfil the same.

While Bahadur Shah, Lakshmibai and Nana Sahib were eager to achieve their political interests, they were not serious towards the hardships of the peasantry and the menial classes. Their unity with the sepoys was also only to strengthen their military positions. Moreover, inefficiency of the rebel leaders against the British was also observed. Obviously, they fought bravely, but it was their strategy that mattered.

Last but not the least important factor was the attitude of the civilians towards the sepoys. The plundering activities and the reckless destruction on their part had alienated the general masses from them. Civil population did not help them at any stage, which was ultimately a factor of the failure of the cause of the revolt.

The Mutiny was suppressed, but it had the long-drawn consequences over the Indian history, which affected almost each and every sphere of life. P.E. Roberts writes, "The suppression of the Mutiny was deemed a fitting time for the Crown finally to take over the control of the Indian government."

The suppression led, on the one hand, to the end of the Mughal rule in India, and on the other of the East India Company, which had established its political authority with the conquest of Plassey (1757). The Company protested against the decision and held that she established the rule in India at a time when the Crown was losing her significant colonial government in the United States.

John S. Mill even filed a petition against the decision but of no use, and the administration passed over to the Crown on November 1, 1858. Sir H.S. Cunningham remarked that it was "a formal than a substantial change." According to the Act of 1859, the Board of Control and the Court of Directors were abolished, and their place was taken over by the Secretary of State for India. The Council of India was formed consistently of seven members. The Indian administration was to be supervised by the Viceroy of the Crown. "For a few years, Crown and Parliament showed a keen desire to supervise

Indian affairs, but this gradually diminished. Towards the end of the sixties hardly a dozen members took any active interest in India." Soon certain factors strengthened the importance of the Secretary of State and his position in the Cabinet increased his authority over the finances and political activities of the government of India.

A very significant aspect of the aftermath of the revolt was the enactment of Indian Councils Act of 1861. As the British had acquaintance of the Indian reaction towards the government's policies, the Indians were nominated to the Legislative Council. The annexationist policy of the East India Company, especially the Doctrine of Lapse, was a prime factor of many States raising the banner of revolt, even though the Company's officials deny this fact. The timely assistance provided by other States helped in crushing the revolt and consequently deeply affected the policy of the Government towards the Indian States during the future course.

Lord Stanley, the Secretary of State for India, expressed his views before the House of Commons: "I think also that the Government, whether in India or in this country, have profited sufficiently by the recent and costly experience, not to feel inclined to pursue that policy of annexation, which, whether well or ill-founded, has undoubtedly, in a great degree, been the cause of the present disaster."

The valuable support of the Indian States had defended the British cause. Sir John Lawrence, the Chief Commissioner of Punjab, reported to Lord Canning, "Had they (the Sikh chiefs of cis-Sutlej territories) deserted our cause any time before the fall of Delhi, the communications with the Punjab would have been cut off.. These chiefs not only remained staunch, but acted vigorously on our behalf." Those who supported the government at this critical juncture were announced many rewards-monetary, territorial as well as titular. To conciliate these Princes, the Queen in her proclamation assured of the safety of their territories and to respect their rights, dignity and honour. They were given the rights of adopting sons and nominating them as their political heirs. Lord Canning realized both at home and in the Council. Metcalfe assesses that "should British power ever in the future be challenged by a foreign foe, or British resources be drained from India to fight a European war, the support of these princes would be worth more to the Empire than any number of British troops."

The revolt had a serious impact on the Indo-European relations, which caused racial bitterness on both the sides. While the Indians were furious over the British atrocities committed on them, the British could not forget the Indians "behaving like brutes and killing English men, women and children" during the days of the revolt.

The Queen had declared that everybody would be granted equal protection of the law and that recruitment to different services and promotions were to be made on the basis of merit, though it was not implemented. The bureaucrats were not willing to treat the Indians on the same footing. Wells, a judge in the Calcutta High Court, explained in the Legislative Council, "It is insulting to place the Europeans on the same level, and subject them to the same regulations as those tainted with the spirit of rebellion.

Between the Indians and the Europeans there could be no equality." The only policy of the British was to increase the respect for the Europeans and to treat the Indians as a subject race. Efforts were made to keep the Indians away from the higher administrative services.

A very serious effect of the revolt was on the Hindu-Muslim relations as well. Though both the communities had actively participated in it, but the Muslims showed more zeal and vigour. The British officers in Agra, Aligarh and Rohilkhand had also reported that the Muslims were "for the most part against us," while the Hindus remained "almost universally friendly." Similar views were held by the Government of Punjab.

On the other hand, the Hindu and the Muslim leaders blamed each other for not extending full cooperation. The British took full advantage of those differences and adopted the policy of divide et imperis. They adopted the strategy of political counterpoises, which continued throughout their rule. All the avenues of progress and enhancement were opened in the Hindu dominated areas, while the Muslims lagged behind in the political, economic and cultural spheres.

The British learnt a lesson from the sepoy mutiny and felt it expedient to do away with the practices originally responsible for it. The Indian soldiers out-numbered their European counterparts by more that 5 times, and some cantonments were held only by the Indians. Consequently, the number of the Europeans was increased to such an extent that they should not be less than half the number of the Indians. Artillery was put strictly under the control of the Europeans. In order to check the possibility of the break-out of any such revolt, the units were divided on communal basis, *e.g.* the Jat regiment, the Sikh regiment, the Gorkha regiment etc. The number of the Brahmans and the Muslims in the army ranks was reduced, while those who had supported the British at this juncture, were recruited in great numbers. Moreover, the sepoys were forbidden to read the Indian newspapers.

Another relatively significant aspect was that the government showed no more interest in the social and religious reforms. It became also very much cautious in extending its support to the Christian missionaries.

The post mutiny period paved the way for the reorganization of the fiscal system. The government's finances were greatly shattered in her efforts to crush the revolt.

Experts in the fiscal affairs were called from England and economic reforms were introduced, which began a new era in Indian economy. Annual budgets, income tax etc. were introduced. Additional taxes, apart from the land-revenue, on the landholders were also introduced.

While free trade policy was adopted for exports on the raw material and tea, the custom duties were reduced on imports. The government undertook the steps to check the expenditures. However, the new commercial policy became highly detrimental to the Indian interest.

Now, the basic aspect of the policy was the economic exploitation by the British as a whole. The Indian trade and industries had already been hampered, and the agriculture ruined. The British now created a wedge among the social classes, appeasing those who could be helpful for the continuance of their rule. The government supported the interests of the landlords and the feudal lords, while divided the peasant by granting certain concessions to the larger peasant farmers, and by enacting laws under which peasant lands could be bought and sold.

The Revolt of 1857 proved to be a turning point in the British rule in India. It was a cumulative result of a number of factors, each having its own importance. The revolt had created a sense of national awakening among the Indians, who in the future raised the banner of independence from the British rule. The revolt had failed in 1857, but it gave many lessons to the Indians to learn from its failure.

7

1857: Mangal Pandey, Rebellious Sepoy

On this date in 1857, ten days before the scheduled date for his execution, Mangal Pandey was hanged at Barrackpore, India, for mutiny against his British officers — a death sentence at the intersection of technology, faith and empire that would prefigure India's first large-scale rebellion against English authority.

For a man of whom much is written and ponderous historical weight is imputed, Mangal Pandey is a mysterious character. Little is known of his life save the very end of it; its significance, as is so often the case, derives from the larger history that preceded and followed it on the subcontinent.

The march of industry was driving better and better ways to kill people, and to this end the British were upgrading old smoothbore firearms with more accurate rifled weapons. Early in 1857, Indian forces got the Pattern 1853 Enfield.

Soldiers of the day loaded their guns by biting open a paper cartridge, which Indian troops had been doing for years. But the Enfield cartridge, coated with a waterproofing grease, smelled or tasted different to many — and rumors spread that it was manufactured with pork lard (which would be an affront to Muslims) or beef tallow (which would be an affront to Hindus).

The British didn't take seriously the potential implications of this postulate among a population already resentful of aggressive Christian proselytizing. When a general petitioned for the expediency of switching back to the old cartridge paper, he got a characteristic response:

"Concessions made to the murmurs and threats of an ignorant race only increase their perversity and folly."

On March 29, Pandey — possibly high — went on a protracted rampage on the parade grounds. The Indian soldiery resisted orders to restrain him, although it also did not answer Pandey's incitement to mutiny, leaving the sepoy to a solitary performance in which he fought off in melee two British officers. Only the arrival of a general — the one who had wanted to replace the cartridges — mastered the situation.

The verdict was a foregone conclusion, but the criminality of Pandey's outburst from the standpoint of the British military is a much easier matter to establish than the chain of events elevating him into national hero. Pandey lived his life forward, but his noteworthiness derives from retrospection.

A month after he hanged, the Indian Rebellion of 1857 broke out, an event (debatably) construed as an Indian War of Independence, dramatically recontextualizing the Barrackpore hanging. His exhortations about the cartridges, about "our religion", suggest him as a like-minded martyr, but there is almost nothing to firmly establish why he did what he did. He even declined to defend himself at trial.

None of this undermines his place in India's national pantheon, and perhaps Pandey's own blank backstory facilitate his mythological adoption. A 2005 Indian film, *Mangal Pandey:*

The Rising, recently placed it on the silver screen, drawing criticism both for naive Indian nationalism and for insufficient reverence for the title character.

Mangal Pandey (1831-1857)

No. 1446 Sepoy Mangal Pandey of the 5th Company, 34th Native Infantary fired the bullet that marked the beginning of the great uprising of 1857. The shot fired at Barrackpore resounded all over the country and soon the cavalry corps at Meerut responded adding a new dimension to the revolt. Twenty six year old Mangal Pande was deeply religious and had a good service record. He was disturbed by some happenings like the court-martial of Jamadar Saligram Singh for refusing to use the greased cartridge and the disbanding of the 19th Native Infantry.

There was also a general feeling among the sepoys that despite long years of loyal and devoted service to East India Company, the 'native' soldiers were unfairly dealt with and treated with arrogance and their genuine grievances were not redressed. After the impulsive act, Mangal Pande tried but could not shoot himself dead. He was court martialled on 6 April 1857. On 8 April, when he was sent to the gallows he was calm and unruffled as befitted a martyr to a noble cause. Ever since the battle of Plassey (June 1757) the Company's territorial power had been growing very fast. By 1818, when the last Peshwa was dethroned, practically all the Indian States had either been annexed or had entered into treaty alliances with the Company on humiliating conditions. The British had become the suzerain power and the Indian princes were mere puppets in their hands.

The policy of expansion did not stop there and the few independent principalities on the frontiers were also annexed whenever an opportunity presented itself. In 1843, Sind was attacked and added to the British dominion; it was an act of wanton aggression to cover the terrible disaster which the

British armies had suffered in the Afghan war. The revolt of Diwan Mulraj of Multan was used as a pretext for the annexation of the Punjab in 1849. The rights of the minor Maharaja, Dalip Singh, who was under the protection of the British, were set aside.

Lord Dalhousie annexed States whenever an occasion arose and often in disregard of solemn engagements. Under his 'Doctrine of Lapse' the princes were denied the long-cherished right of adoption; in this way Dalhousie annexed the Maratha States of Satara, Nagpur and Jhansi and several minor principalities. On the death of the ex-Peshwa, Baji Rao 11, the pension granted to him was abolished and the claims of his adopted son, Nana Dhondu Pant, were disregarded. In 1856, the kingdom of Oudh was annexed. The Nawabs had been the faithful allies of the Company for a long time; but such considerations did not weigh much with Dalhousie, who had a calculated plan to abolish all the Indian States.

The result of his policy was that no Indian prince felt secure, and there was widespread resentment. The annexations also caused discontent among the subjects of the dispossessed princes, as they were bound to them by old ties of tradition. For an Englishman like Dalhousie it was not possible to realize that the people had genuine respect for old dynasties and that they might prefer the old tyranny to the oppression of the new rulers.

The ever widening frontiers of the Company's dominion also resulted in the shutting out of Indians from all avenues of honourable employment. The administrative reforms of Cornwallis, introduced at the close of the 18th century, meant the virtual exclusion of Indians from high posts. The administration assumed an English character. There was perhaps no other case of foreign rule in which the people were "so completely excluded from all share of the government of the country as in British India". To make matters worse, the English administrators gradually became arrogant and there was a wide gulf between them and the people. They could hardly know the feelings of the vast multitude, which providence had placed under their rule.

Reason of the Sepoy Rebellion 1857

In February, 1857 the Sepoy companies was the issued the new gunpowder cartridges for the Enfield rifle and then British officers offered them that provide to a new cartridges for use to the Hindu or Muslim both, but that cartridges they are not accepted because this made from cow and pig fat and this is forbidden in Hinduism, while consumption of Pork is 'haram in Islam'.

Britain gained after the British two-thirds of India's land, and imperialism had started to affect every Indian's life (whether by technology like the telegraph, evangelical missionary efforts, or legislative area efforts, or administrative and land ownership reform). There is only need of some tiny spark to set off a great revolt, but there was an only incredible amount of worries.

Before 1857 Sepoy rebellion was not minor outbreaks within his Sepoy rank. But this had been at suddenly and quickly. 'Spark' came to begin this period of revolts was the introduction of new, and it also became breech-loading Enfield rifle.

In Meerut, the first event was the boldly and cruelly at the garrison in which European was found murdered by the mutineers. Then they marched to Delhi and "placed themselves under the leadership of the impotent and bewildered Mogul Emperor Bahadur Shah." Throughout May and June in the India, if mutiny spread through the gang's Valley, the Rajputana, Central India, and parts of Bengal. Cawnpore has surrendered to Nana Sahib, and Lucknow, the only British had the outpost in Oudh, was besieged on June. At Cawnpore discovered the 200 European men, women, and children had murdered a month earlier and the mutiny and siege on July

17. Suspected mutineers were tied to cannons and executed when vengeance was swift and harsh. When Mutiny had broken then again, British power restored.

The Sepoy rebellion would always be remembered late by some Indian Freedom fighters as the first stages of struggle for independence from colonialism.

History of Rebellion

Mangal Pandey was a great rebellion of the India, On 29 March 1857, At the barracks near parade ground, near Calcutta, 29-year-old Mangal Pandey of the 34th BNI. Mangal Pandey angered by the recent actions of the East India Company. Then he declared he would become a rebel for India. And fight against the commanders. Major James Hewson has informed about Mangal Pandey behavior for sergeant then he decides to shoot to the Mangal Pandey.

General John Hearsey came out to the Parade ground to investigate to the Mangal Pandey who was involved in of 'religious frenzy.' He gives ordered to quarter guard Jemadar Ishwari Prasad to arrest him, but the Jemadar was not arrested to him and become refused. Then the quarter guard and other Sepoy rebellion present the single exception of a soldier called Shaikh Patlu for an arrest to the Mangal Pandey.

Shaikh Patlu has restrained to the Mangal Pandey from continuing attack.

An open and active Mangal Pandey have failed to incite his comrades. Mangal Pandey tried to save his life, by placing his musket to his chest and pulling the trigger with his toe but he managed only to wound himself. After two days he was hanged at the ordered off court-martialled on 6 April.

Jemadar Ishwari Prasad hanged on 22 April. The regiment was disbanded and stripped of its uniforms because it was felt that harbored ill feelings towards its superiors, individually after this incident. Shaikh Patlu performance promoted to the rank of Bengal army.

Sepoy in other regiments thought this punishment very harsh. During the formal disbanding helped foment the rebellion of some view of the demonstration of disgrace. Disgruntled ex-Sepoy returned home to Awadh with a desire for revenge.

Civilian Disquiet

There was so much own rebellion and more multifarious. There is a further type of rebellion such as feudal nobility, rural landlords called Taluqdars. Here presented the nobility of who had lost titles and doctrine of lapse, which refused to recognize the adopted children of princes as legal heirs, felt that the company had interfered with the traditional system of inheritance.

Civilian rebellion such as Nana Sahib and the Rani of Jhansi belonged to this group; They fought with the British company for freedom, and they were prepared to accept an East India Company.

Understanding 1857

The Revolt of 1857 had as its opponent what was the largest colonial power of the world. It has, therefore, a notable place in the history of Imperialism, and no study of the Revolt can be separated from that of the emergence and internal mechanics of Imperialism. In a letter (27 October 1890) to Conrad Schmidt, Engels noted that while colonial powers before 1800 aspired to capture sources of imports at the lowest cost, thereafter following the Industrial Revolution, they essentially sought markets for their own industrial manufacturers. In respect to India, Marx (New York Daily Tribune, 11 July 1853) dated the change to 1813, when the Charter Act threw Indian markets open to British manufactures by abolishing the East India Company's commercial monopoly.

The results of this invasion of 'Free Trade' for India's own artisanal manufactures were disastrous. In Capital, I, (ed. Dona Torr, p.461), Marx noted that after 1833, there came about "the wholesale extinction of Indian handloom weavers", amounting to a "destruction of the human race." It must be remembered that this new source of misery was in addition to the increasing burden of 'Tribute', extracted by Britain through excessive over-taxation of the country. Marx had seen in such Tribute a special source of primitive accumulation for British capital; and this too was, therefore, an inseparable element of the new regime of Free Trade, how much individual Free Traders like Bright may have criticised it.

Not only was 'Free Trade' a vehicle for the conquest of external markets by British capitalism, a new impetus was now given to world-wide expansion of British power, so as to impose 'Free Trade' on the whole world. 'Imperialism of Free Trade' is how this new aggressive stage in British colonialism has been described by British historians, J. Gallagher and R. Robinson in an essay of this title (1953). Marx himself had never believed in the sincerity of the 'peace cant' of the British Free Traders (Tribune, 11 July 1853) and spoke specifically of the military means that were adopted for "securing the monopoly of the Indian market to the Manchester Free Traders".

The expansion of British power, both world-wide and within the Indian subcontinent imposed a still further burden on India: Annexations of princely states came one after another: Sind, Punjab, Nagpur, Satara, Jhansi, Awadh, all went into Britain's grasp between 1844 and 1856. In each state large sections from courtiers to common people lost their means of livelihood. Payment had to be made in blood as well. The Bengal Army became a major instrument that was put to use for fulfilling the sub-continental and global ambitions of British imperialism. The bones of thousands of its Sepoys lay scattered in the fields of Afghanistan, Sind, Punjab, Burma, Crimea and China, and no end to the blood-letting was in sight when the storm burst over the greased cartridges in 1857.

We can thus see in 1857 a critical juncture in the history of emerging Imperialism: the pressures it relentlessly exerted on the largest colony in the world, provoked, finally, an anti-colonial outbreak, unique for its scale in the whole of the nineteenth century. The rebellion pitted against the colonial regime over 120,000 trained professional soldiers from the Bengal Army, the most modern army east of Suez, with tens of thousands of other armed rebels, reinforcing and aiding them. In terms of the area affected, nearly a fourth of the population of British India (some five crores of people) passed under rebel control.

That the Revolt of 1857 had its roots in the pressures exerted on India by the Imperialism of Free Trade can hardly be denied; but the depth and breadth of the upheaval also raises the question of the classes and groups that became involved in it, and of their grievances and aspirations.

In his Discovery of India (1946) Jawaharlal Nehru wrote most feelingly about the slaughter and suffering imposed on the people of India by the British during and after the Revolt; and he compared the 'racialism' exhibited by the British to that of Hitler. Yet he simultaneously believed that the uprising was essentially "a feudal outburst, headed by the feudal chiefs and their followers, and aided by the widespread anti-foreign sentiment". Nehru repeats this characterisation at the end of his account of the rebellion as well.

Such characterisation, though perhaps natural with the limited amount of evidence available on 1857 at the time Nehru was writing, needs now to be reconsidered.

In the first place, the perception inexplicably overlooks the role of the Bengal Army sepoys. Coming largely from peasant and small land-owing families, they had been drilled and trained in modern warfare and, often themselves literate, were attuned to the mode of British administration with its committees and councils. They had thus no "feudal" attachments that we can think of. Yet, they remained from the beginning to the end, the firmest single component among the ranks of the Rebels. During the rebellion, they asserted their 'democratic' attitude by electing their officers (with, often enough, largely Hindu regiments electing Muslims, and vice versa). They formed 'councils' to govern their affairs, and in Delhi established the famous 'Court of Administration.' If their officers gave themselves designations, they were those of a modern army; such as "Captains", "Colonels" and "Generals"!

Another class, which we tend to overlook, is that of the educated in the towns, who were increasingly affected by modern ideas. While it is true that there was nothing comparable to the Bengal Renaissance in the Hindustani-speaking zone, at both Delhi and Agra colleges had been established, imparting modern education. In People's Democracy (April 23-29), Shireen Moosvi has given an account of weekly newspapers coming out in Delhi during the time it was held by the rebels (May-September 1857). Her account shows clearly that the rebel newspapers addressed themselves to people at large, and were not mere Mughal court bulletins.

Let us take a cursory view of the Delhi Urdu Akhbar (June 21,1857), where under the heading "Seize this Opportunity", it tells its readers that the English had been depriving India of its wealth, by taking it away to England, and remarks upon how the new rebel administration, as it extended its control over "districts" would open opportunities for men of "education and capacity." It calls upon the scions of the old aristocracy to leave their ways of idleness and take to various trades and crafts. It especially commends the ironsmiths who were manufacturing "rifles, English guns and Turkish pistols." Its appeal to Hindus and Muslims to fight the English does, indeed, make use of the slogan of saving both religions from the onslaught of the alien English, but it increasingly shifts to patriotic sentiments, addressing "fellow countrymen" and glorying in the exploits of "the Indian Army" (Fauj-i-Hindustani).

Modern methods of propaganda were also employed: a pamphlet containing an appeal to Hindus and Muslims was separately printed to be sold at a quarter Rupee per copy (issues of 5 and 12 July). Interestingly, the paper's hero consistently is not any of the Mughal princes, but the brusque "republican" sepoy leader, the Commander-in-Chief, "General" Bakht Khan. Clearly, the weekly's readership consists not just of the dependants of the Mughal court, but also a much larger educated population, which was being invited to support the rebel cause by enticing vistas of what they would gain from an Indian (not necessarily, a mere Royal) regime. The general slaughter by way of retribution carried out by the English in Delhi after its fall in September proved that in English eyes the rebel appeals to the Delhi citizenry for support had not fallen on deaf ears.

Beyond the educated class, there were the artisans whose callings the Delhi Urdu Akhbar in its issue of 21 June had so much commended. These included many who had lost their employment owing to the competition of British manufactures, especially textiles. Firuz Shah, the famous rebel leader, in his Proclamation of August 25, 1857–which reads surprisingly like a modern political party's programme–makes a special promise of giving employment to the weavers and other kinds of artisans rendered unemployed by English importations.

Such artisans formed another class that turned out to be strongly sympathetic to the rebellion. Syed Ahmad Khan then a British agent, in his contemporary memoir of the Revolt in district Bijnor (Sarkashi-i-zila' Bijnor) speaks sneeringly of how the sepoys and professional soldiers of the local rebel leader, Mahmud Khan were reinforced by "cottoncarders and weavers, who had hitherto handled only yarn, and never a sword."

While we are discussing the outlook of the rebel press at Delhi, it may be mentioned that none of the extant issues of the three weekly newspapers display the slightest sign of Wahabi influence. Iqtidar Alam Khan's critique of the theory of a large Wahabi role in 1857 is going to be published in a subsequent issue, so more need not be said here about it. The practical absence of theocratic influence on rebel leaders, despite the constant cry of religion in danger is, indeed, remarkable.

As for peasant support for the rebellion this became so immediately apparent that already in his article in the Tribune (16 September 1857), Marx was drawing a comparison between the Indian Revolt and the French Revolution of 1789, on this, very basis. The peasants were hard-pressed by the Mahalwari system of land-tax (a consequence of the British pressure for Tribute), and the Revolt gave them an opportunity to throw off the tax-collector. The late Eric Stokes deserves much gratitude for his detailed studies of peasant participation in the Revolt. To him is owed the telling quotation from the report of Mark Thornhill (15 November 1858), where that official held "the agricultural labouring class", *i.e.* peasants, rather than "the large proprietors", as having been "the most hostile" to the continuance of British rule during the Revolt.

That large numbers of zamindars, the bulk of Oudh talluqdars and some princely courts threw their lot with the Rebels is, on the other hand, quite undeniable; and Talmiz Khaldun's suggestion that the 1857 Revolt was developing into "a peasant [and, therefore, anti-feudal] war against indigenous landlordism and foreign-imperialism" was rightly contested by P.C. Joshi in whose centenary volume on 1857 the essay had appeared. Much of the visible rebel leadership came from these elements: the reluctant Bahadur Shah Zafar, Nana Sahib and Tantia Topi, Hazarat Mahal and her entourage, Khan Bahadur Khan of Bareilly, Lakshmibai of

Jhansi, and Kunwar Singh and Amar Singh of Jagdishpur, all came from what one can conveniently characterise as feudal classes. Most of them had their own grievances, over lost rights or rebuffed claims. But it needs to be borne in mind that resistance and struggle, in which support had more and more widely to be sought from among the common people, could not but force fundamental changes of outlook. One may look, for instance at two proclamations of Birjis Qadr, whom the rebels declared to be the ruler of Awadh.

The first was the proclamation of Rebel Rule at Lucknow, printed in Urdu and Hindi side by side, and issued in June 1857. Addressed to the "Zamindars and the Common People of this Country" it blames the English for their attack on the religion of both Hindus and Muslims, on their seizures of land, and on their disregard of the dignity of the higher classes by treating them at par with the meanest! There is no explicit reference to India, in the main text and, quite clearly, the interests of the landed aristocracy are given primacy. Contrast this with the last appeal to the Indian people in reply to Queen Victoria's Proclamation of November 1858. In this Appeal issued on behalf of Birjis Qadr, India (Hindustan) is in the forefront. The story is briefly narrated of how the British by force and fraud have acquired territory after territory in India from Tipu's Mysore to Dulip Singh's Punjab. The rebels are not to believe in Victoria's honeyed words, but to continue the struggle. Victoria's Proclamation shows, it asserts, that if British rule continues, Indians would remain mere hewers of wood and drawers of water. The petty matters, such as the loss of hierarchical dignity, are here quietly forgotten.

One must recognize that the overall historical orientation of the 1857 Revolt cannot be established in definitive terms for the simple reason that, because of its ruthless suppression, there is no way of knowing how it would have developed should success have come its way. But some preliminary suggestions can still be made.

Given the crucial role of the Bengal Army sepoys in initiating and carrying the Revolt forward, the Revolt at least drew on one element of the 'regenerative' process, that Marx had spoken of, in his seminal articles of 1853 on British rule. The Sepoys did not at all belong to the old world of princes and landlords. Significant also are the early traces of modern ideas and perceptions that we see in rebel journalism of Delhi and certain proclamations of the rebels.

The fact that these modern or quasi-modern elements could make common cause with princely courts, zamindars, unemployed artisans and overtaxed peasants was due to a particular combination of circumstances created partly by that transformation of colonialism itself, with a discussion of which this essay had opened. To characterise the revolt as either "feudal" or "bourgeois" would be unhistorical. The time for one was past, the time for the other had not come. Such discussions have their place in attempting any understanding of how 1857 came about.

But what cannot be disputed is either the sheer patriotism of so many, whatever class they came from, or their undying defiance in the face of so brutal and ferocious a retribution as the English visited upon them. The memory of the Rebels' sacrifices in what they believed so ardently to be the cause of their country will remain ever green in our people's memory— so long, as the royal poet of 1857 said, as "the country of India endures."

The Causes of The Rebellion

Maj (Retd) Agha Humayun Amin from Washington DC Gives a Brilliant Analysis of The 1857 War of Independence

The events of 1857 were unique both in terms of historical precedence and in terms of the socio-political sphere as far as India was concerned. India as a region has known foreign invaders more frequently than any other region in world history. The reason for it does not lie in the docility or weakness of the Indo-Pak people but in the peculiar geographical position of India by virtue of being bounded in the north by a vast inhospitable and unproductive region which starts from beyond the Indus valley and stretches far north into the steppes of central and eastern Asia.

It is an irony of history that the east Asian tribes and races forced the west Asian nomads of Mongol and Turk origin to seek their barbaric design for plunder westwards and these central Asian people repeatedly invaded India. In the process these central and north east Asian nomadic people conquered and colonized China also but also extended their sway in South Asia as well as West Asia.

The first important aspect of the whole affair is to broadly analyze the conduct of the races who conquered India. This is a relatively simple exercise. Starting from the Aryans, Huns, Greeks etc. the invaders of India can be classified into two broad categories *i.e.* 'Settlers' or 'Plunderers'. The settlers were the ones who came to the country, conquered it and settled here. They can be compared with Normans or Saxons who went to Britain and gradually got assimilated in the country which they had initially conquered. The 'Plunderers' were the ones who came like 'Ghaznavis', 'Mongols', 'Nadir Shah', 'Ahmad Shah Abdali' etc. looted the country and went back to their country of origin.

For those who do not know Indian history it is important to specify that the first Muslim invaders of India *i.e.*, the 'Arabs' were settlers and not plunderers. They conquered and annexed a part of India and made it a province of their empire. Mahmud of Ghaznavi was both a plunderer and a settler. Initially his concentration was on simply acquiring the material wealth which during that age was done by 'Plunder'. Subsequently geographical and logistical factors forced him to also act as a part settler and thus he made present 'Punjab' and 'Frontier' a province of his empire. But even then area east of west Punjab remained his area to be plundered. The

'Ghauri' Turks who were 'Muslims' by religion were the first Muslim settlers in India east of Indus valley region. They made Delhi their capital and gradually got assimilated in India. They were followed by various Muslim dynasties of Central Asian or Afghan/Pathan origin who may be classified as usurpers.

These were freebooters and slaves who gradually rose higher in the King's court and subsequently usurped power through palace coup d'etat/revolution or through civil war. The only exception to these settlers was Tamerlane who sacked and destroyed Delhi in 1398 and did not establish a dynasty in India.The relevance of discussing only the Muslim invaders of India prior to the British while omitting pre-Muslim invaders is simple. In 1857 people belonging to three religions or three broad groups who were fighting with certain objectives. These were the British, the Hindus and the Muslims. It is in this context that an endeavour is made in these paragraphs to acquaint only the layman reader about the broad mechanics of Indo-Pak history

The last settler-invaders of India prior to the British were the Mughals. They came to India in 1526. They defeated the then Pathan Muslim King of Delhi at Panipat and established the Mughal dynasty. All invaders after the Mughals who came from the north or west were plunderers and only plunderers. These include 'Nadir Shah' and 'Ahmad Shah Abdali'. In justice to Ahmad Shah Abdali it must be stated that Ahmad Shah Abdali in 1761 did want to become a settler and establish his dynasty in India but he failed to do so because his soldiers had rebelled and demanded a return back to Afghanistan. All Muslim invaders who attacked India from the north did not distinguish the Hindus from Muslims and subjected all Indians to indiscriminate looting.

For a casual reader of history in this light the British may also appear as just one of the earlier invaders of India. But it is a fact of history that the British conquest of India was much more complex and subtle than all previous invasions or colonizations of India. Four features make it different: (1) The Third Religion Factor. (2) The Communication Factor. (3) The Economic Factor. (4) The Organizational Factor. India's history prior to Plassey was relatively simple. Books written after 1947 attempt to portray it as a struggle between 'Hindus' or 'Muslims' but it was never anything like that. But then historians are prisoners of time and the society they live in at least in the vast majority of cases. Those who endeavour to write history as it happened do so at the risk of their life or loss of social approval or just because they are not bothered or pushed about pleasing the majority. The struggle in India prior to 1757 and even after 1757 was between individuals who were 'Muslims' or 'Hindus' by pure chance and who manipulated their followers or subjects in a certain direction guided and propelled not by any religious convictions but by personal whims and subjective designs. 'Religion' was just one of their tools, a political expedient, a wartime slogan, a matter of policy.

Muslims killed Muslims and Hindus killed Hindus for simple power or for patronage or economic benefit. Hindus killed Hindus for Muslim Kings and Muslims killed Muslims for Hindu Kings. Everything was mixed, diverse and complex. Rajput Hindu Generals fought for Aurangzeb against the Hindu rebel Shivaji. Aurangzeb preferred to ennoble Mahratta Hindus who formed 16.7% of his nobles in the period (1679-1707) than lets say 'Punjabi Muslims' who were not even 2%. Thus Hindu Rajputs and Hindu Mahrattas were the bulk of Aurangzeb's nobility and their number in the period (1679-1707) stood at 31.6 % 32.

Thus we see that in the period between 1526 and 1707 the India of the Mughals was a state which had opened its doors to the 'Natives' as the British later degradingly referred to the Indians. The British who became a force to reckon within India after 1757 brought a totally new phenomena to India *i.e.*, 'slavery' and 'subjugation'. An 'Indian' could be a common soldier or a non-commissioned officer or a junior commissioned officer but remained junior or subservient to the junior most British officer who may have been a cook or son of a cook in Britain! The civil servants, the governors, all ranks and appointments of any consequence were open to only the white man.

This was a new experience for the Indians. They had been colonized by the Aryans, the Greeks, the Arabs, the Turks, the Pathans. But all these people had either plundered them and left or if they had stayed, they always allowed the native Indians to be a part of the dominant classes. The problem with the British was that they thought that they were very special whereas India had been conquered even by 'Horse Thieves' and central Asian adventurers who could not fight with the Uzbeks! The Indians were surprised and disillusioned and there grew a feeling in north India that these new invaders were different. If we glance at Indian history between 1757 and 1857, we find hardly any Indian in a respectable official rank or position in the territories governed by the English East India Company.

Whereas if we compare this with lets say the Mughals we find that the third Mughal Emperor Akbar just about three decades after his grandfather Babar had established the Mughal Empire in India was freely employing Indians both Hindus and Muslims in all the ranks and appointments of his army and civil service. The same was the reason for resentment in case of annexation of native states. It closed all doors of advancement to an Indian in any profession/service.

The British were different not because they were racists or fascists but because of the circumstances in which history had placed them. We will take the first of these *i.e.*, 'The Religion Factor'. Before 1757 all contenders in Indian politics were either Hindus or Muslims. But this was irrelevant because both the parties used religion just as one of the means to a personal or political end. Shivaji later eulogized as a Hindu freedom fighter was in service of a Muslim state. Aurangzeb's most famous general Jai Singh was a Hindu Rajput. Ahmad Shah Abdali later on portrayed as a purely Muslim hero could find no better governor of Muslim majority Lahore than 'Kabuli Mal' a Hindu! Ranjit Singh's (the Sikh hero) most trusted advisors were the Muslim Fakir brothers of Lahore. Now suddenly after 1757 a third religion 'Christianity' appears on the Indian scenario.

The British were 'Christians' by accident and religion was an insignificant factor in their list of priorities. But the very fact that there was a third religion made the scenario complex. New probabilities and possibilities opened for political leaders, religious thinkers and all those who held positions of power or patronage. Had the British assimilated like the earlier conquerors their religion would not have been given much importance. But since their conduct was discriminatory and biased 'Christianity' also became an issue. The new possibility that the Hindus and Muslims could combine against a common enemy provided a good propaganda theme for manipulators (politicians) for purpose of political propaganda. This is ironic since 'Islam and Christianity' have many things in common. But even then between 1757 and 1857 most of the conflicts were between states and groups in which Muslims frequently allied with the British and the British frequently allied with the Hindus or Muslims against other Muslim states or other European powers.

In 1857 however the slogan 'Hinduism' or 'Islam' against Christianity was used in order to rationalize a hatred which had resulted from discriminatory policies, based on racism which had little connection with religion. Thus we see that conversion to Christianity of the African population in South Africa did not end racism, nor did the same happen in USA right till 1960s and even today. 'Religion' was not an issue in itself but the EEIC policy of discrimination made it an issue and 'Religion' in a symbolic sense was used as a slogan by the freedom fighters' leaders in 1857.

The second factor which made the British different from all other previous invaders was the communication factor. England was many months journey by sea or overland from India but the 'sea communications' which the British used were guaranteed and reliable by virtue of British naval mastery established after 1588 and consolidated as a result of a series of naval victories in the 17th, 18th and 19th centuries. Thus reliable/guaranteed communications kept the British in touch with the home country. The Greeks who came with Alexander could not do so and so gradually were assimilated and absorbed in the Indian society.

The Mughals also could not maintain direct contact with their home country since they themselves had been expelled from their home country by the Uzbeks. The Mughals did employ many men of Turko-Mongol origin but political expediency and the demand and supply gap both necessitated a nobility drawn from a diverse array of Persian Afghan/ Pathan and selected Indian background. In the British case the communication factor made it different. Had the Mughals reached India by sea from a far off island and had good naval commanders like Drake, Rodney and Nelson they may also have behaved differently! Thus reliable overseas communications ensured a constant supply of manpower for lower intermediate and higher military civil and political jobs. Britain at this time was experiencing a population boom and India was an opportunity for many Britons who may have ended unemployed or in debtor jails had they stayed in Britain.

The third factor was the economic factor created because of trading objectives and the industrial revolution. The English East India Company's presence was based on trade between India and Britain and pure business or economic activity confined to India only was not their sole objective. India was a base for raw material which had to be transported to Britain. This necessitated economic exploitation and discriminatory taxation and commercial regulation. The English East India Company in this aspect was a prisoner of circumstances and its consequent unpopularity in the Indian populace was regarded by its British Directors sitting in London as a necessary evil. In this aspect, the East India Company was a sophisticated version of Mahmud Ghaznavi or Nadir Shah or Shivaji or Ahmad Shah Abdali. These honourable gentlemen graced the scene for a short duration and then left. The East India Company was there to stay.

The fourth and the most crucial factor which made the British racist and discriminatory and thus different from all previous invaders of India was the 'Organizational Factor'. The Mughals who came to India from Central Asia were exiles or political refugees. Their first founder King Babar could not hold his ancestral state 'Ferghana' in Central Asia. He crossed the Oxus and went southward into present day Afghanistan where he established a new Kingdom. Subsequently he came to India, defeated the reigning Pathan Muslim King of Delhi, and then decided to stay on in India although he detested India's hot weather just like the English East India Company's officials later on. Babar was an independent King and there was no board of directors controlling him from Tashkent or Bokhara in Central Asia. He had decided to stay in India and his descendants never thought like an Englishman of 19th century that one day they would go back and live in a palace or cottage in Central Asia. This was so not because they disliked Central Asia but because it was not economically viable or safe to go and live there. Babar, the founder of the Mughal Empire despised native Indians just as much as many arrogant officials of the English East India Company. But Babar's descendants had no option but to employ Indians in their army and civil service keeping in view the dictates of their situation by virtue of logistical political and social necessity.

The Britisher who came to India in 1757 or in 1847 was not always a racist. Many of them married here, intimately mingled with Indians, took a deep interest in Indian history and made very positive contributions in the literary, social, educational and economic spheres. But all said and done these Britishers were servants of a company which had its headquarters in London, where all policies pertaining to general operations, legislation, recruitment etc. were made. Even if they wanted to, they could not follow a policy which was fair and just for the Indian natives.

The British parliament had many Indian lovers in its ranks but these legislators could not directly interfere with the government of the East India Company. Lord Dalhousie, one of the Governor Generals in India wanted for example to include Indians in the higher government of India but his wish was overruled by the court of Directors of the English East India Company. During the discussions while drafting the India Act of 1853 in the British Parliament a proposal was made to have Indian members in the viceroy's legislative council. This proposal was defeated due to opposition on part of Sir Charles Wood who stated that 'No two Indians could be found to represent adequately the diversity of Hindu and Muslim society'. There was an element of truth in Charles Wood's argument but it was just a minute fraction of the truth against the whole argument in favour of having Indian members. Later on after 1857, the British by and large accepted it as one of the principal causes of the rebellion of 1857. Sir Syed writing in the post-1857 era declared 'Exclusion' as the principle cause of the rebellion.

Lord Macaulay a man who is very often grossly misunderstood and unjustly criticized in India and Pakistan was a matter of fact a great advocate of inclusion of Indians in the higher ranks by virtue of allowing them to compete in the open competitive examinations. Macaulay had been trying to promote the Indian cause since 1833-36. He laid the foundation of modern education in India.

However, in sum total the 'organizational' factor was the

principal cause of the deep British-Indian divide which led to the events which erupted like a volcano in 1857. This 'Discrimination' was a major underlying cause of the rebellion of 1857. It was this 'Discrimination' which compelled Indians to think of the British as alien exploiters. It led to exclusion of Indians from the higher legislative and political forums and thus contributed to evolution of laws which were perceived by Indians as an attack on caste and religion.

The Policy of Annexation

The policy of annexation and conquest has also been widely pointed out as one of the principal causes of the rebellion of 1857. This aspect is not as simple as it appears at first sight. The standpoint from which it is mostly condemned is morality or moral grounds but there is no morality in empire building or politics. The policy of annexation on part of the English East India Company was nothing but a logical outcome of superior military strength. The British victory at Plassey had made the English East India Company de facto master of Bengal, Bihar and Orissa. The abolition of the Nawabi in Bengal made them the de jure master also in 1765 or in 1773 technically speaking. By 1764 after having won at Buxar from the political and military point of view the English East India Company (EEIC) was the master of north India at least as far as all territory of the Oudh state extended.

The EEIC could have annexed Oudh in 1765 but they did not do so in 1765 because they assessed that it was practically not possible for them to manage this vast territory. But they started the process of annexation in 1775 when the Nawab of Oudh agreed to cede to the EEIC territories comprising Benaras, Jaunpore, Mirzapur etc. held by Chait Singh as a subsidiary of the Nawab. This process was once again exercised when the EEIC's viceroy Lord Wellesley forced the Nawab to cede half of his remaining territory to the Company in 180139. This led to extension of EEIC authority to half of northern

India as far as eastern boundary of Aligarh district and all territory east of Ganges river. As a matter of fact, Lord Wellesley was planning to annex whole of Oudh state in September, 1801 when for this purpose he had sent his brother Henry Wellesley to the state's Capital Lucknow However long negotiations followed in which the viceroy's brother agreed to cession of only half the territory to the EEIC's domains.

This annexation rendered Oudh politically geographically and militarily little more than a petty vassal state of the East India Company. The probable reason why the viceroy's brother agreed to only half the territory appears to have been partly a fear that complete annexation may be perceived as politically inexpedient being a violation of 1798 between Sir John Shore and Oudh. The EEIC had guaranteed in this treaty that it would protect Oudh in perpetuity. There are two aspects of this annexation. From the strict legal point it can be criticized as unjust. However from the political military or economic point of view it strengthened the EEIC's position in northern India. It brought a vast increase in land revenue since the land revenue was approximately 13,523,474 rupees. Militarily it rendered Oudh incapable of concluding an effective alliance with the Mahrattas or another power since now Oudh was surrounded on all three sides by EEIC's territory whereas previously the EEIC territories were only on its eastern borders.

An interesting fact to be noted here is that the EEICs acquisitions from Oudh in 1801 comprised almost half territory which had initially been assigned by the Mughal Emperor Shah Alam to EEIC in 1765 *i.e.* the Kora and Allahabad areas. This also included Rohilkhand which had been conquered by the Nawab of Oudh by employment of EEIC's Bengal Army brigade which the Nawab had hired in 1774. But this is not the appropriate place to go into any further details. Our aim is to debate the influence of the EEIC's policy of annexation as a subsequent cause of the outbreak of the 1857 rebellion.

We see that the EEIC annexed half of Oudh state whereas

they were initially planning to annex the whole of it. It was the viceroy Lord Wellesley's decision and was approved by the Board of Directors. Oudh's army also as per this agreement was to be reduced to less than one tenth of its previous size. Viewed from the political and strategic expediency point of view this treaty was a masterstroke.

In the long term, it laid the foundations for future war against the Mahrattas in the North and against Sikhs and Afghanistan subsequently. How should we view this action today? Keeping in view the origins of the Oudh Nawab we see that his ancestors were the governors of the Mughal Emperor in Oudh. Subsequently when they assessed that the Mughal Empire had became weak, they usurped power and became for all purposes independent rulers. Militarily they were convincingly defeated by the EEIC at Buxar in 1764. But after Buxar the EEIC did not annex Oudh because Lord Clive felt that it was too big to be practically controlled or managed by the EEIC, keeping in view the EEIC's organization and potential at that time. The EEIC resident was not far from the truth once he explained to Nawab Saadat that 'These countries did not belong to your ancestors but were added to the family possessions by the power of the British arms'.

There was however one subtle contradiction in all this. All things said and done Oudh remained an independent and comparatively peaceful region at a time when, most of other parts of India including Delhi, Punjab and Central India witnessed considerable bloodshed, anarchy and destruction. Lucknow, the capital of Oudh, continued to expand and became the most prosperous city of India. New palaces continued to be built, roads were constructed and widened and the people of Oudh had a pride which was much more than inhabitants of any part of India except the Hyderabad state, another British lackey in the south. Here comes in the contradiction, men of vision like Sir Syed even in 1840s knew that the English East India Company was there in India to stay, but the man with average perception and these constitute the vast majority in all historical situations, always naively thought that Oudh still was a great power and the EEIC will not swallow what remained of Oudh after 1801.

The military lessons of Buxar figured nowhere in the minds of the large majority of the population of Oudh. We see exactly the same phenomena in Germany after 1918 once the German populace mistakenly believed that they had never been militarily defeated but had been stabbed in the back. Myths in themselves are nothing but once whole nations believe in them, the consequences can be disastrous. The Pakistani public was at a loss once they learnt from the terms of the peace agreement of Tashkent that the impression that Pakistan had won the war of 1965 was false.

We are discussing Oudh in considerably greater detail because it was in this region that the rebellion of 1857 came closest to what we call a 'Peoples War'. Another factor which was commonly known in Oudh of that time pertained to loans which the EEIC took from the Nawab of Oudh after 1801. These were less loans and more of a forced exaction since the Nawab clearly knew that in case he refused a loan the EEIC may use force in order to make him pay. There are three aspects about the loans. From the strict pragmatic and expediency standpoint the EEIC was squeezing a docile vassal who they had militarily defeated and who was under their political bondage. Secondly, from the strictly moral or emotional point of view the conduct of the EEIC was regarded by the people, the nobles and the king as blackmail. This added to the prevailing hatred against the EEIC.

The third aspect is the Nawab's behaviour. The Nawab's sole interest was to stay in power. Had he taken a resolute stand and resisted the EEIC's unjust or unfair demands we could have said that he was a hero. But the Nawab's sole interest was in his personal comfort, his concubines and in his debauchery. Here a sharp distinction has to be drawn. The ruling house led by the Nawab had little to do with patriotism or any other lofty moral ideals. Their sole motivation was self-interest. Militarily they had lost the contest in 1764. EEIC's agreement to let them rule stemmed not from any fear of the Nawab's military might but from a simple pragmatic assessment in 1765 and even in 1801 that Oudh was too large a morsel to be swallowed in one go. The EEIC was above all a commercial organization and thoughtless, unplanned impulsive expansion figured nowhere in the principles which guided its foreign policy in India. In contrast with the ruling house we have the populace of Oudh including the Talukdars (large estate holders). This group was a better lot as compared to the Nawab.

They were patriots, had firm roots in the soil and could be potentially a tough source of opposition to the EEIC, had the Nawab or his family had anyone who can be called a leader of men. But alas! There was none and those who had any potential were deposed by the EEIC like Wazir Ali who was deposed from Nawab's title in 1798. It is important to note that the vast majority of Oudh's Talukdars were Hindu Rajputs. Wazir Ali unlike most of Indian rulers after 1757 was surprisingly a true patriot. He succeeded his father Asif-ud-Daula who ruled Oudh from 1775 to 1797 in September, 1797.

The Wazir Ali episode is not directly connected with the events of 1857 but my purpose in relating it here is to acquaint those readers who are not aware of this incident about the self seeking and ulterior motives of majority of Indian rulers in the period 1757-1857. Wazir Ali was claimed to be his son by Asif-ud-Daula and was generally acknowledged to be so by the vast majority in Oudh at least till 1797 when he succeeded his father Asif-ud-Daula as Nawab of Oudh in September 1797. Whether he was or not is a minor issue once we view Wazir Ali as a true patriot. But there is one thing we know with certainty, that once the EEIC discovered that Wazir Ali was anti-EEIC and wanted to strengthen his army they immediately started digging facts to prove that Wazir Ali was a bastard, since the late Asif-ud-Daula was impotent! Wazir Ali immediately after his assumption of power had annoyed his nobles by declaring his intention to reduce their power. He also wanted to reduce the influence of the EEIC's Resident at Lucknow who were performing the same role as Ambassadors of some so-called super powers perform in today's third world countries.

The nobles immediately started their intrigues and urged the EEIC Resident to depose Wazir Ali. Sir John Shore, the Governor General received a divine revelation that Wazir Ali was an illegitimate son! EEIC lackey Saadat Ali Khan who was half brother of Wazir Ali's father and had been fed on crumbs thrown by the EEIC for some 20 years in form of a pension also played an instrumental role in this affair. Saadat Ali Khan had attempted to overthrow his half brother, Asif-ud-Daula in 1776 and once his attempted coup failed he sought asylum in EEIC territory. The EEIC gave him asylum and assigned him a handsome pension. Saadat Ali Khan intrigued with the EEIC in late 1797 and a bargain was struck. Initially the EEIC demanded cession of more territory in return for placing Saadat Ali as Nawab. Subsequently this was changed to financial exactions and handing over of the impregnable and strategic Allahabad fort to the EEIC. Saadat Ali's elevation to the rulership of Oudh was the result of acceptance of a humiliating treaty consisting of 23 articles which further weakened Oudh. The Company was now solely incharge of the external defence of Oudh.

The annual subsidy which Oudh had to pay was increased to 76 lakh rupees. The Oudh army for internal security was now not to exceed 35,000 men. Oudh could no longer have any contact with any other foreign country and was barred from allowing any European to either serve in its army or even to settle in Oudh without the EEIC's permission. Thus we see Saadat Ali, a pensioner of EEIC residing at Banaras being informed about his elevation to the Nawabi of Oudh. Saadat Ali travels to Kanpur and from there is escorted to Lucknow by EEIC's troops and is proclaimed Nawab on 21

January, 1798.

But this is not the end, it is the same Saadat Ali who again yields to the EEIC half more of Oudh in 1801. Wazir Ali was exiled to Banaras from where Saadat Ali came to assume Nawabship. The EEIC however was not happy to allow Wazir Ali to stay so close to Oudh's border. They, therefore, resolved in end of 1798 to transfer him to Calcutta. Wazir Ali resisted this attempt and in this connection visited the British Resident a certain Mr. Cherry on 14th January 1799. Mr. Cherry reportedly raised his voice during the course of discussion upon which Wazir Ali lost his temper and struck Mr. Cherry with his sword. This was a signal for Wazir Ali's armed retainers to attack which they did killing the Resident Mr. Cherry and four other Englishmen.

The fifth Englishman in that room managed to escape 49. Wazir Ali fled from the scene, raised an army of 6,000 but was defeated. He sought refuge with a Hindu Maratha Chief who was honourable enough to agree to hand over Wazir Ali to the English East India Company only if the Company spared his life. The Company kept its promise. Wazir Ali was shifted to Calcutta from Banaras in 1800 and died a natural death in March 181750. The English Company was more honourable than some third world armies of the post-1947 who first swored on the Holy Quran to do the same as in Wazir Ali's case and later handed some insurgents to the EEIC. The Wazir Ali affair was used by the new EEIC Viceroy Lord Wellesley to pressurize Saadat Ali to disband his army and to replace it by a pure EEIC force.

The writing that the EEIC wanted to annex whole of Oudh was on the wall right from 1775 when they took Banaras from Oudh. It became clearer in 1797 during the Wazir Ali affair and by 1801 it was crystal clear. The Oudh Nawabs made the EEIC designs easier by gross mismanagement and debauchery. From 1798 to 1856 their guiding principle of conduct was to somehow stay in power, however much

Oudh is reduced in sovereignty or territory or in financial terms. The EEIC did not end the matter of exactions in 1801.

In 1814 they again interfered with succession to Nawabship on Saadat Ali Khan's death and placed the candidate of their choice Ghaziuddin Haider on the throne. The price of this succession was forced loans to the EEIC by Oudh on extremely low interest rates. Thus Ghaziuddin Haider loaned the EEIC some 3.085 million Pound Sterlings during his reign from 1814-2753. Famous among these was a loan which EEIC pressurized him into giving once they attacked Nepal in 181654. Ghaziuddin was also influenced by the EEIC viceroy Lord Hastings into declaring himself King in 1819 and thus theoretically setting aside his political subservience to the Mughal Emperor at Delhi.

Practically the Mughal Emperor was also an EEIC pensioner56 from 1803 once the EEIC captured Delhi but theoretically EEIC was his subject and servant. Here it is interesting to note that Tipu Sultan had also declared himself King repudiating the Mughals and had acknowledged the Sultan of Ottoman Turkey as the Caliph of Islam. Similarly Shivaji had declared himself a King, independent of the Mughal empire in second half of 17th century. It is interesting to analyze EEIC's subsequent excuse in 1856 of citing mismanagement in the final annexation of Oudh.

As a matter of fact it was the policy of forced loans which destroyed the economy of Oudh. These loans were exorted from Oudh at 5% to 6% rate of interest which at that time was considered very low since from 1793 the EEIC had been paying its shareholders 10.5% per annum. The first loan of 1.85 million pounds was taken in 1814. The second of 1.00 million Pound Sterlings in 1815 and the third of 1.00 million Pound Sterlings in 1825. The second loan was never repaid and instead a worthless part of Terai forest territory taken from Nepal was given to Oudh. The same territory was returned to Nepal in 1858 59 as a reward for sending a force to assist the EEIC in the final capture of Lucknow in March 1858.

In 1837, the Governor General Lord Auckland forced on Oudh a treaty by which it asserted its right to take over what remained of Oudh if the Company felt that the country was being mismanaged. The treaty also imposed on Oudh an annual payment of 1,600,000 Rupees. This last clause was in violation of treaty of 1801 by which the Company had agreed to defend Oudh in return for cession of half of its territory. Even the Board of Directors of the EEIC viewed this treaty as unjust and unfair and declared it null and void. The Governor General however never informed the King of Oudh that the treaty was entirely annulled. He only informed him that he would not have to pay for his defence. King Muhammad Ali Shah (1837-42) continued to appease the EEIC. In around 1839 he granted them a loan of 3,240,800 Rs. at 4% interest. In 1842 he again loaned the EEIC 1,400,000 or 140,000 Pounds at 5% interest.

These two loans were exorted to make up for the disastrous First Afghan War. It is significant to note that all interest which the EEIC paid back to Oudh was used for pensions and allowances of the Oudh Royal Family. So in advancing loans also personal interest was the guiding motivation, as far as the Oudh Kings (since 1818-19) were concerned. Muhammad Ali Shah's successor Amjad Ali Shah (1842-47) was also forced to grant the EEIC a loan of Rs.3,200,000 on his accession in 184262. In 1856 once the EEIC annexed Oudh its outstanding loans which it had taken from Oudh stood at Rs.35,000,000 or 3.5 million Pounds. The purpose of this considerable attention devoted to the EEIC conduct in Oudh may seem a little too detailed. It is however important since it illustrates bad faith and greed on both sides and the sufferers in this case were the common people.

The year 1848 was an important year for India. It was in this year that the 36 years old Lord Dalhousie came to India. Dalhousie was a utilitarian and progressive man. He rightly viewed the princely states of India as an unnecessary anachronism. On 18th September 1848 he in a letter said, 'I have got two other kingdoms on hand to dispose of, Oudh and Hyderabad'. But this was not all, Dalhousie went further and he made another profound observation which convincingly proves that Dalhousie had a remarkable insight about the character of the Indo-Pak rulers of that time. This observation was true not only for the king of Oudh but for almost all Indo-Pak rulers of that time and to a certain extent even those of today in many third world countries. Dalhousie thus wrote about the king of Oudh 'The king won't offend or quarrel with us, and will take any amount of kicking without being rebellious!'. Thus Dalhousie made a firm resolve to annex Oudh.

In 1849, Dalhousie appointed Sleeman as Resident of Oudh. Sleeman was instructed by Dalhousie to prepare a report on the existing affairs of Oudh. Sleeman by his deep knowledge of India and its languages was ideally suited for this task. Born in 1788, Sleeman joined the East India Company's Bengal Army as an ensign in 1810 at Allahabad Fort. He fought in the Anglo-Nepalese War of 1814-16. He became famous for the decisive part he played in suppression of 'Thugs' in India from 1826 to 183265. Sleeman's report was published in 1851. He agreed to the fact that Oudh was mismanaged but also expressed his opinion against annexing it. With profound insight, Sleeman warned Dalhousie that Oudh's annexation would have a very negative effect on Bengal Army, bulk of whose Sepoys belonged to Oudh. Sleeman actually warned Dalhousie that annexation of Oudh would lead to a mutiny in the Bengal Army. The next Resident James Outram who succeeded in 1854 also prepared another report largely based on Sleeman's report. Outram also agreed with the 'mismanagement' concept but was not in favour of outright annexation. Outram favoured a regency council led by the EEIC who would reform Oudh's state of affairs. Dalhousie prepared a minute on the 'Oudh' question in which he recommended that entire administration should be taken over by the EEIC while the king of Oudh should be allowed to retain his title.

The viceregal council of Dalhousie was however against violating the 1801 treaty which guaranteed the sovereignty of Oudh. The difference of opinion however was resolved by the EEIC court of Directors and the British government's decision to annex Oudh. Wajid Ali Shah resisted the decision but was forced to abdicate and Dalhousie issued a proclamation dated 13th February 1856 through the medium of which he declared annexation of Oudh to the territories of the EEIC. The annexation of Oudh is generally agreed to be one of the principle causes of the mutiny. This was not true. As we shall see later that the rebellion began from Meerut and Oudh followed the lead given by the Meerut Troopers only after two months! What was true was the fact that the rebellion lasted for a far longer time because bulk of the Bengal Army was recruited from the Hindu Rajput and Hindu Jat population of Oudh. This was why the struggle in Oudh did come closest to the modern conception of people's war in 1857. It did take the EEIC almost one year to recapture Oudh. The reason for this protracted affair was concentration of some 80% sepoy regiments in Oudh and the immense pride of Rajput Talukdars.

The foremost cause of resentment in the people of Oudh against the EEIC was its extortionist policy from 1775 onwards. The EEIC to a considerable extent rightly accused the Oudh Nawabs and subsequently its kings of misgovernment and mal-administration. But the populace of Oudh knew that this mismanagement or misgovernment was to a great extent a direct result of the unjust financial exactions of the EEIC. And yet the EEIC annexed the state in 1856. Inwardly or militarily Oudh may have been very weak but culturally or symbolically Lucknow of 1820s or 1830s had outshone Delhi. It was a modern city of palaces spacious gardens and paved road. The nobles and a large part of populace were prosperous and owed their prosperity to Oudh being an independent state.

The king had an army and a host of other officials numbering more than 1,60,000. On annexation most of these were rendered jobless. Heavy tax was imposed on opium which was a very frequently used drug.

This enraged a considerable part of the populace. Land deeds and titles of ownership were subjected to scrutiny and zealous young civil servants of the EEIC in a bid to emancipate the peasants annoyed the Talukdars (Jagirdars or big landlords). This phenomenon was paradoxical, since the British intention in this case was positive but the landlord of that day had a much greater influence and, this the British agreed to accept at the cost of enlightenment of the people of the subcontinent after 1857.

Thus, though 1857 which in itself was a positive affair resulted in retarding growth of progressive ideas in India which men like Dalhousie wanted to advance. Thus after 1857 the British Government which assumed the Government of India decided to ally with the feudals whereas before 1857 their predecessor the EEIC were following an excellent policy of destroying feudalism in India. There were cases where estates were rightfully held but the proofs of ownership were missing. Confiscation of these estates also alienated a large number of landowners in Oudh. Even if the annexation of Oudh itself was not a negative step, the conduct of many officials of the EEIC alienated a vast majority of the populace. Sir James Outram the Resident at Oudh who had been appointed the Chief Commissioner on annexation of Oudh was a reasonable man.

He was however forced to leave for England due to illness. His successor a certain Mr. Coverly Jackson who was only the officiating Chief Commissioner was a very short-tempered and irrational man. His arrogant and racist behaviour immediately alienated all those people who came into contact with him. The conduct of the EEIC officials was careless and irresponsible and in the process made the EEIC administration more unpopular. For more than an year through sheer carelessness and negligence the allowances were not paid to pensioners which was part of the EEIC settlement terms. Covertly Jackson occupied the palace which had been earmarked for the Oudh Royal family.

The EEIC committed yet another significant tactical blunder. Dalhousie had given detailed instructions to Outram regarding disarming the populace of Oudh who at the time of annexation were well armed since in those days security of the common citizen or village was their own affair. Outram however did not carry out this order since he felt that it could be done after the summer. Dalhousie in a demi official letter addressed to Outram in 1856 had thus written, 'It is my intention that not a single fortified place should be left in Oudh with the exception of those that belong to Government.

It is further my intention that the whole population should be disarmed... as was done with such excellent effect in the Punjab in 1849'. This disarming was as a matter of fact not carried out and thus prolonged the war of independence in Oudh till almost 1859. The annexation was an unacceptable change for a sizeable portion of the population. Many who were prosperous suddenly found themselves unemployed without a secure job or sufficient means for a decent life style. The Bengal Sepoys who belonged to Oudh were a privileged class in Oudh since they were EEIC employees. They were given a preferential treatment in their private dealings with Oudh state officials once they visited their houses and villages on long leave. Now they were just like any other common man living in Oudh. Thus a sepoy noted that 'I used to be a great man when I went home, a servant would carry my bags, the rest of the village rose when I approached. Now the lowest puffs their pipes in my face'. In sum total the net situation in 1856 was explosive in Oudh in particular and Northern India in general.

Bibliography

Allen, Charles, *Soldier Sahibs: The Men Who Made the North-West Frontier,* London: John Murray, 2000.

Amin, Aha H., *The Sepoy Rebellion of 1857-59: Reinterpreted,* Lahore: Strategicus and Tacticus, 1998.

Anderson, Clare, *The Indian Uprising of 1857-8: Prisons, Prisoners and Rebellion,* London: Anthem Press, 2007.

Chakravarty, Gautam, *The Indian Mutiny and the British Imagination,* Cambridge University Press, 2005.

Chaudhuri, Sashi Bhusan, *Civil Rebellion in the Indian Mutinies 1857-1859,* Calcutta: World Press Private, 1957.

D'Oyly, Charles, *Eight Months Experience of the Sepoy Revolt in 1857,* (1891; repr. Uckfield: Naval and Military Press, 2006.

D'Souza, Shanthie Mariet. *"Mangal Pandey: Indian soldier". Encyclopaedia Britannica.*

---- *Mangal Pandey: True Story of an Indian Revolutionary,* 2005, Rupa & Co. Mumbai

---- Saul David, page 70, "The Indian Mutiny", Penguin Books 2003

Dalrymple, William. *The Last Mughal: the fall of a dynasty: Delhi, 1857.* NY: Alfred A. Knopf, 2007.

David, Saul, *The Indian Mutiny: 1857*, 2002; London: Penguin, 2003.

Durendra Nath Sen, page 48 *Eighteen Fifty-Seven*, The Publications Division, Ministry of Information & Broadcasting, Government of India, May 1957

Edwardes, Michael, *Red Year: The Indian Rebellion of 1857*, (London: Hamish Hamilton, 1973.

Farooqui, Mahmood, trans., *Besieged: Voices from Delhi 1857*, (London: Penguin, 2010.

Fitchett, W.H. *A Tale of the Great Mutiny.* London: Smith, Elder & Co., 1911.

Forrest, George W., *A History of the Indian Mutiny 1857-58*, (3 vols, 1912; repr. New Delhi: Asian Educational Services, 2006.

Fremont-Barnes, Gregory, *The Indian Mutiny 1857-58*, (Oxford: Osprey, 2007.

Gupta, Pratul Chandra, *Nana Sahib and the Rising at Cawnpore*, (Oxford University Press, 1963.

Harris, John, *The Indian Mutiny*, (1973; repr., Ware: Wordsworth Editions, 2001.

Hibbert, Christopher, *The Great Mutiny: India 1857*, (London: Viking, 1978.

Ireland, W. W., *History of the Siege of Delhi*, (1859, repr. Uckfield: Naval and Military Press, 2006.

Kaye, John, and Malleson, George, *History of the Indian Mutiny*, 1890; Cambridge University Press, 2010.

Kaye, Sir John & G.B. Malleson, *The Indian Mutiny of 1857.* Delhi: (1st edition 1890) Westport, CT: Greenwood Press, reprint 2005.

Keay, John, *The Honourable Company: A History of the English*

East India Company, London: Harper Collins, 1993.

Khan, Sir Syed Ahmad, *Asbab-e Baghawat-e Hind* 1859; Translated as *The Causes of the Indian Revolt.* Allahabad, 1873.

Littlewood, Arthur, ed., *The Indian Mutiny and Beyond: The Letters of Robert Shebbeare VC*, Barnsley: Pen and Sword, 2007.

Majumdar, Ramesh Chandra, *The Sepoy Mutiny and the Revolt of 1857*, Calcutta: Firma K. L. Mukhopadhyay, 1963.

Mangal Pandey breathes life into Barrackpore's past, samrat ray, 1 December 2008, merinews.com

Marx, Karl, and Engels, Friedrich, *The First Indian War of Independence 1857-59.*

Masters, John. *Nightrunners of Bengal.* New York: Viking Press, 1951.

Metcalfe, Thomas R., *The Aftermath of Revolt: India, 1857-1870*, Princeton University Press, 1964.

Misra, Amaresh, *Lucknow: Fire of Grace: The Story of Its Renaissance, Revolution and the Aftermath*, 1999; New Delhi: Rupa, 2004.

Mukherjee, Rudrangshu. *Awadh in Revolt 1857-1858.* Delhi: Permanent Black, 2001.

--------: *Mangal Pandey: Brave Martyr or Accidental Hero?*, New Delhi: Penguin, 2005.

Nayar, Pramod K., *The Penguin 1857 Reader*, New Delhi: Penguin, 2007.

Omissi, David, *The Sepoy and the Raj: The Indian Army, 1860-1940*, London: Macmillan, 1994.

Palmer, J. A. B., *The Mutiny Outbreak at Meerut in 1857*, Cambridge University Press.

Pandey Sita Ram. *From Sepoy to Subedar, Being the Life and Adventures of Subedar Sita Ram, a Native Officer of the Bengal Native Army, Written and Related by Himself*, trans. Lt. Col. Norgate, Lahore: Bengal Staff Corps, 1873, ed. James

Lunt, (Delhi: Vikas Publications, 1970).

Pati, Biswamoy, ed., *The 1857 Rebellion*, (Oxford University Press, 2007.

Raikes, Charles. *Notes on the Revolt in the North-Western Provinces of India*. London: Longman, 1858.

Roy, Tapti. *The politics of a popular uprising: Bundelkhand 1857*. Delhi: for the Oxford University Press, 1994.

Sir John Kaye & G.B. Malleson: *The Indian Mutiny of 1857*, Delhi: Rupa & Co. 2005.

Stanley, Peter. *White Mutiny: British Military Culture in India, 1825-1875*. NY: New York University Press, 1998.

Stokes, Eric. *The Peasant Armed: The Indian Revolt of 1857*. Oxford: Clarendon Press, 1986.

Index